Cancer Diaries *of an* Ultra Runner

*Best Wishes
Sandra
x*

Sandra Tullett

Cancer Diaries of an Ultra Runner

Copyright © 2024 Sandra Tullett

Published by Compass-Publishing UK 2024
ISBN 978-1-915962-33-1

Cover photography © Ben Langhorne, SussexSportPhotography.com
Photos © Russ Tullett, Paul Mason, Sarah Dryden, Alan Dunk,
Stuart March, Nici Griffin, Chris Gambs, Sparta Photography Club
and David Brawn

Edited and typeset by The Book Refinery Ltd
www.TheBookRefinery.com

The right of Sandra Tullett to be identified as the author of this work has been asserted by her in accordance with the Copyright, Designs and Patents Act 1988.

All rights reserved. No part of this publication may be reproduced, stored in a retrieval system, or transmitted, in any form or by any means (electronic, mechanical, photocopying, recording or otherwise), without the prior written permission of the publisher.

A CIP catalogue record for this book is available from the British Library.

*To my husband, Russ, I am forever grateful for
every extra day I get to spend with you.
I love you more!*

*To my son, John, you make me proud every single day.
With all my love.*

Contents

Foreword	7
Prologue	9
Introduction	15
Chapter 1 – Discovery and Surgery	22
Chapter 2 – Post Surgery and Pre Chemotherapy	46
Chapter 3 – Cycle 1	66
Chapter 4 – Cycle 2	80
Chapter 5 – Cycle 3 / Thames Path 100	88
Chapter 6 – Cycle 4	109
Chapter 7 – Cycle 5 / Purbrook Ladies 5	127
Chapter 8 – Cycle 6 / North Downs Half Marathon	134
Chapter 9 – Radiotherapy	143
Chapter 10 – Getting Back to Normal	154
Chapter 11 – This is Sparta!	165
Epilogue	173
Acknowledgements	176

Foreword

by James Elson, *Founder of Centurion Running*

In a line of work that involves organising very long distance trail running events, I have been fortunate enough to meet some incredible people from all walks of life. People who have faced tremendous adversity and forged a path forward through sheer will and determination.

Essentially, many thousands of examples of the incredible spirit of endurance that underpins us as the human race.

When I first met Sandra, her lust for life, vibrancy and ability to communicate warmly to everyone and anyone within the running community were immediately evident. It was clear she had a consistently positive outlook. But perhaps more remarkably, she was willing to share a natural anxiety towards the challenges she optionally faced through the incredibly difficult events she chose to test herself against. She was able to see each situation for what it was. Both extremely difficult, but also a challenge that she could overcome.

But the magic in her words resonated as soon as I picked up this book. It is a rare ability to be able to share oneself so openly as Sandra does consistently from first to last through these pages. And together with her incredible resilience, she is able to tell us her story and to tell it in a way that is simultaneously poignant, empathetic and incredibly valuable.

Sandra's background as a runner is worthy of a book by itself. Someone who has run well over a hundred marathons, scores of ultramarathons and pushed themselves time and again in training, can lean on a raft of tales that will keep the reader entertained for hours. Indeed, many have written books about individual feats of endeavour far inferior to the one she sets out to tell us about in the opening pages – the Thames Ring 250.

Where her story gains its true magic, however, is with the additional challenge of cancer. What she has provided here through her words is a gift to anybody experiencing adversity.

There is a deep synergy between her life as a runner and her approach to tackling cancer, and it's the interweaving of that story that is so gripping and useful, firstly to those faced with similar challenges, but ultimately to us all.

Several things resonate above all in her words. The clarity of thought she is able to maintain as she takes us on a journey via her diary through the entire process of diagnosis, treatment and recovery from the disease. How running is always there for her, the thing that allows her to maintain mental focus. I haven't read a more compelling reason to be a runner than Sandra is able to communicate here.

But perhaps more than anything, far from being afraid to embrace the details of intimate conversations with her husband, Russ, as well as the physical and emotional reality of dealing with cancer, she embraces it all and tells us just how it is in such a completely relatable way.

Sandra's story is a compelling narrative of resilience, recovery and the pursuit of a seemingly insurmountable goal – or rather goals in terms of her races and her disease. Her candid account exemplifies the way triumph can emerge from the crucible of adversity.

Her story is an exploration of the human spirit and a profound meditation on perseverance, passion, and the relentless pursuit of the extraordinary. If we could all take an ounce of the pragmatic, empathetic and stoic approach to such a shocking and difficult challenge, we would be far better off.

My own personal thanks to Sandra for being brave enough to tell this story and for being such a pivotal part of our community, in both running and beyond.

Prologue

Thames Ring 250, June 2017

'Sometimes, you never know the value of a moment until it becomes a memory.'

'I'm done! I don't want to do this anymore.'

I'm on the phone to my soon-to-be husband, Russ. It's 9:30pm and I have been awake for almost 36 hours. I'm walking along the Grand Union Canal on a mild Thursday evening in June. My feet are sore, and my right ankle hurts. Every step I take is painful. I am meant to be running, but I can't run anymore. I have been walking for what seems like hours, towards the Milton Keynes checkpoint. It is under a bridge somewhere, but it feels like it's taking forever to get there. I just want to reach the checkpoint and stop. I'm exhausted and I've had enough.

Russ ignores my moans and tells me that everyone he's seen arriving at Milton Keynes looks exhausted and ready to quit. He tells me that I will be OK after a sleep. I'm not interested in his theory. He does not feel like I do. I decide that once I get to the checkpoint, I will stop and go home.

A few weeks earlier, Russ and I had come up with a plan to ensure I completed the Thames Ring 250-mile Ultra Race. We agreed that my only reasons for stopping before the finishing line would be if I needed an ambulance or if I was timed out due to going too slow. However, I was no longer interested in our plan. I had covered 130 miles, but I still had 120 to go. How could I finish feeling this wretched? I couldn't run anymore. I could carry on walking, but my ankle and feet were too sore to go all that way, and besides, I would be timed out anyway for being too slow.

Finally, I reached the checkpoint. As soon as I arrived, Russ ignored all my protests and pushed me into one of the small tents that had been erected under the bridge for weary runners to sleep in. He brought my sleeping bag to me, pulled off my shoes and, whilst zipping up the tent, sharply told me to get some rest. I climbed into the sleeping bag, but I could not sleep because of my uncontrollable shivering. I rang Russ from the tent to say that I was too cold. He put some hot water in a bottle for me to use as a makeshift hot water bottle. My husband's actions saved my race.

Altogether, I spent three hours at the checkpoint, most of it in a tent either asleep or trying to sleep. Russ was right. When I woke up, I felt so much better. The lack of proper rest had made it hard to think clearly. A race medic strapped up my swollen ankle, put tape on my sore soles and advised me to wear my laces much looser.

Somewhere in the early hours of Friday morning, I set off again. My feet and ankle felt so much better, and I found that I was able to run again. I had paid the price for going too fast in the early stages and not getting enough sleep, but fortunately, I had time to make up for my mistakes. I had already decided that I was not here to race. I was here for the experience of running a 250-mile ultra-event with a 100-hour cut off. Provided you kept within the race time cut offs at each checkpoint you could continue. I had worked out that if I could manage to run for the first day or two then I would be able to finish, even if I had to walk the rest of the way. Although the available time is generous, typically, only 40% of participants reach the finish line. Ultimately, blisters, injuries and lack of sleep lead to runners dropping out early.

I went back on my way without any further negative thoughts. No doubt this was partly due to the accumulating lack of sleep robbing

Prologue

me of my capacity to think clearly. I just kept moving forwards, like a zombie, incapable of the level of analysis that might make me consider whether this was a bad idea. I spent most of the journey walking on my own, day and night, except for one morning when I lost my phone and had to temporarily borrow one from another runner. We ended up walking off the course together to buy a bacon roll at the railway station in Banbury, before re-joining the route and separating again for the remainder of the race. It all felt very surreal. I was hardly able to run, but that didn't particularly bother me. I knew I was inside the cut offs, and that at the next checkpoint I would be able to take a 20-to-30-minute break.

On day four, when I knew I was likely to finish, I remember walking along the canal in the brilliant afternoon sunshine when a couple of women on a barge asked me what I was doing (I had to wear a race number on my front the whole time, which made me highly conspicuous). I broke down in tears when I told them. They were tears of happiness and disbelief that I was doing this amazing thing, and they reminded me that these memories were exactly why I had chosen to take part in this event.

As the night drew in, I reached Oxford and got back on the Thames Path. I was now last in the race, with a couple of runners slightly ahead of me. By now, the lack of sleep was taking its toll and, as I walked to Abingdon, I started to hallucinate. The leaves looked like dragons. I would bend down, look more closely and think, *Wow, that's amazing.* But strangely, I never felt scared. I also started talking to the person next to me, only to realise I was all alone. I had a tracker on me, which Russ regularly checked to make sure I was still moving. Right then, the trail floor looked really appealing, but I managed to resist the temptation to have a lie down.

I finally reached Abingdon around midnight. I wasn't really aware of what was going on, but Russ persuaded me to sleep for a short while before waking me abruptly in the early hours so I could continue the race alongside two other runners rather than on my own. His thinking was that we could all support each other for the last leg. I also remember Russ getting me to eat something straight after waking. 'Is this breakfast?' I asked him, feeling confused all over again. But as I slowly woke up and my brain cleared, I realised this was the last day and I only had 18 miles to go. The other two runners and I left in the darkness of the early hours of day five and stuck together for the last part of the route. Despite enjoying the days and nights I had spent on my own, sharing this section of the race felt very special. I couldn't have asked for better companions than John and Mike. We pushed each other when we felt we needed to run to keep ahead of the cut off and we looked out for each other – and laughed – when clambering over stiles and up and down steps. There was even a scary moment when we decided we needed a nap and settled down for a few minutes in a field. We must have made a very odd sight. I thought one of them was keeping a check on the time and they thought I was, yet none of us were. It was lucky we managed to wake ourselves up or our race could have ended right there in the field!

As we neared the end, I spent some time listening to music through my headphones and reflecting. When we reached a sign that said 2.5 miles to go, we stopped and hugged each other. We walked the last part, savouring our final moments while knowing we would finish before the 100-hour race cut off. We ran over the last bridge to the finish line hand in hand.

My reason for doing the event was to create special memories and to experience the journey rather than to race it. Just finishing would be a massive achievement, and one that no one would ever be able to take away from me. No matter what happened to me in life, I would be able to say, 'I did that!'

Prologue

In August that same year, Russ and I married. My feet had just about recovered enough to get into my wedding shoes. It was the best day ever.

You never know what is waiting for you around the corner, and just five months after completing the race, I was diagnosed with breast cancer. The end of the year had an entirely different challenge in store. But whatever the future held, I still had a Thames Ring 250 medal on display in a large frame on the wall alongside my race number and pictures of me at the finish line. My wedding photos were also on the wall to remind me of our beautiful day. I have made many precious memories in my life, but by the end of 2017, having seemingly unlimited time to make more was no longer a certainty.

Introduction

You never think it will happen to you until it does.

Cancer touches everyone eventually, whether it is a friend who is diagnosed, a close family member or you. The disease is everywhere. When you settle down to watch the television, a *Stand Up To Cancer* fundraising programme will remind you that one in two of us will get it in our lifetime. We think it is something that happens to other people, and that we are somehow immune, but this isn't the case.

I am now part of these statistics, and I have had to come to terms with this fact. The false belief that it would never happen to me meant that my diagnosis stopped me in my tracks. It was like a massive slap in the face. A wake-up call, a reality check. Suddenly, my normal, safe life was turned into one full of turmoil and uncertainty. The first time I sat in front of the doctor and she uttered the words, 'I'm sorry but you have cancer' was completely and utterly devastating, yet somehow it *still* didn't feel like it was really happening to me. I would swing between disbelief, acceptance and fear. For the first time, I was faced with my own mortality, and it was both shocking and terrifying. Then I was thrown in at the deep end of a new life full of appointments and treatment plans. Over those initial few weeks, the pace of change was relentless. The effort of having to deal with other people's emotions as well as my own was utterly exhausting. It consumed everything, and I was caught up in a life that was tumbling out of control, dragging me down like a sinking ship, and with my loved ones in tow, who were also having to come to terms with these changing circumstances. I was someone's daughter, someone's mum and someone's wife with cancer, and this was hard for my family to take in, so I had to help them navigate this new path whilst also finding my own way along it.

From my own personal experience, and from reading the experiences of others via the support groups I joined on Facebook, I've learnt that this is often how those first days and weeks after the initial diagnosis feel. What helped me and many others was finding a way to take back some control. For me, running was my saviour. It gave me something to get up for each morning. I entered an ultra-running event called Autumn 100, which coincided with the end of my treatment, and this kept me moving forward rather than sinking into the sofa in despair and self-pity.

When I was first diagnosed, I didn't think I would be able to run whilst undergoing treatment. I had heard many stories of people throwing up and experiencing other awful side effects from the chemotherapy, which meant they weren't even able to get up in the morning. However, shortly after my diagnosis, a friend told me about someone she knew who had run the Great South Run, a 10-mile race in Portsmouth, while she was undergoing treatment. This planted a seed for me, and I began to consider the possibility of exercising through my treatment. When I asked a breast care nurse about this, I was assured that staying active was a good idea.

The current recommendation is to aim for 20 minutes of aerobic exercise at least three times per week while undergoing cancer treatment. It is said that physical activity can help reduce fatigue and bring back the patient's sense of control. Research has shown that exercise is 'safe, possible and helpful' for many people with cancer. It can help improve the body's response to treatment, no matter what the stage or type of cancer.

Introduction

So, I decided that I would try to run throughout my cancer treatment.

But I don't usually run just a few miles each week. I am an ultra-runner, and my weekly mileage is typically between 40 to 50 miles, which increases a few weeks before a big event. An ultramarathon, or 'ultra', is defined as any footrace event that exceeds 26.2 miles (the standard marathon distance). This means that an ultra can be any distance from 50k (31 miles) to 100 miles, and even beyond. There are 48-hour events and six-day events. There is even a 3,100-mile race that lasts several weeks and comprises 5,649 laps of one extended city block in Queens, New York.

I began running initially to aid my chosen sport of rowing. Rowing was in the family. My brother competed internationally, and my dad was involved in the sport his entire life, initially as a competitor and later helping to run many of the larger rowing events. As I progressed in my teens, running became an inevitable part of my exercise regimen. My rowing club was near Barnes Bridge, along the River Thames, and I would run with my team upriver and over Twickenham Bridge, and then downriver and back over Hammersmith Bridge. I had no particular interest in running at this time, it was just a necessary part of my training.

I stopped rowing when I started university, but I kept up running and would go around two to three times a week. This led to me running my first half marathon in the New Forest, despite my longest training run being about eight miles. It took me over two weeks to recover from the ordeal. I continued to run for several years after that, albeit sporadically.

I ran more regularly after moving to Plymouth in 1992, when I was 27, but this was generally on my own and going no farther than the distance of a half marathon. I progressed from this when I moved to

Portsmouth in 2000 with my first husband and our seven-year-old son, John. I formed many friendships at my local Portsmouth Joggers running club, and it's this camaraderie that has kept me running ever since.

Initially, I had no intention of ever running a marathon. However, I ran with the club's marathon training group at the weekends and talked to friends after they had completed their race, which made me think that perhaps I should give it a go. My first one was the D-Day Landings Marathon in Caen, France, in 2004. It was a very hot day and I found it extremely challenging. I came through the finish line crying my eyes out, overcome with emotion at achieving this significant milestone. As is often the case after completing your first marathon, I said 'never again', but it wasn't too long before I felt ready to enter another one. I continued running a marathon or two each year until 2009, when I dipped my toe into ultra-running. Initially, the events I ran were less than 50 miles. I ran my first 50-mile event, the North Downs 50, in 2012.

Having divorced in 2007, I met my current husband, Russ, at the end of 2013 at my local Portsmouth running club. He had dreams of running a 100-mile event and entered the South Downs Way 100 for June 2014. Unfortunately, he could not take part in the race as he was struggling with his knees. I ran the race instead but found that by about 40 miles in, I was beginning to feel nauseous. I had never felt like this before. The sickness gradually worsened until I could no longer keep any food down. By the time evening came, after being on my feet and running all day, I was completely depleted and could barely put one foot in front of the other. There was no way I could finish. I sat down near a checkpoint next to Russ, all ready to quit. Russ said that if I wanted to give up then I had to go to the checkpoint and hand my number in myself. He knew how much finishing the race meant to me, so he wasn't going to make it easy for me to stop. He showed me messages from the many friends who were supporting me, including one that said, 'She is strong, she has enough time to walk to the finish, she can do it.' After sitting down for over an hour and refusing to get up, the sickness subsided a little and the messages of support spurred me on. I got myself back running again and continued the race. With 15 miles to go, having got through the night, I became very sick again. I cried with frustration and utter exhaustion. But the new day, Russ's encouragement and the support of my friends helped me to keep going to the finish. Completing my first 100 miler was an utterly amazing feeling. The nausea and despair of the previous day were already forgotten and in its place were feelings of euphoria and peace.

Since then, I have continued to enter ultra runs each year, some of which are even longer than 100 miles. I still find that I get nauseous, but this is a common affliction for many who do this type of event. I found that if I ran slower my stomach would be under less stress and I could cope better. I ran the 130-mile Liverpool to Leeds canal race in the summer of 2016, and at the end of that same year, I ran the Portsmouth Coastal Marathon with Russ, to celebrate completing my 100th running event of a marathon distance or more.

Running an ultra is filled with highs and lows. When you feel good, you know that it won't be long until you feel awful again. When those dark moments arrive, you must persuade yourself that you will soon come out the other side. This is not easy when you are utterly exhausted and feel completely broken. You cannot eat, you have blisters, and you ache so much that moving forward can be a mere shuffle rather than a run. Your mind, in its bid to protect you, tries to convince you that it would be far better if you just stopped. You tell yourself that giving up won't matter, even though deep down you know that you will regret it the next day. I have had a few experiences of failing to finish, which is commonly known as a DNF. At the time you feel that stopping is the only option. However, when you look back you wonder if there were things you could have done differently to keep yourself going, and you draw on this knowledge the next time you run. You try new ways to try and prevent the sickness, blisters and injuries. You keep going because you know that the reward of success after surmounting these various obstacles will be so much sweeter. With ultra-running, every single event brings you something new to learn.

Going through cancer treatment was a daily fight. A fight against the side effects of the poison that was coursing through my body and a fight against the fatigue that threatened to stop me getting out of bed in the morning and getting out the door. Each day I put my running gear on was about me taking back some control over what was happening. Running gave me purpose and something to focus on. It also gave me something to aim for when all the treatment was over. It can so often feel like the end is a long way away. Taking each day at a time and getting out for a run kept me moving forward. If I could not run, then I would walk instead.

There were times when I could not run. As the treatment progressed, the side effects became more difficult to overcome. Before being diagnosed, I kept a log of my running, and as I started my treatment, I continued this as a diary. There were many mornings when I woke up early either due to worry or because the medication I was taking caused insomnia. So, I would get up and start documenting what was happening to me each day. In addition to my running, this diary became my therapy and I continued to write it until after my treatment finished.

Despite my mileage being more than the average runner, I hope my experiences show what can be done. It is possible to exercise through cancer treatment, and it can be a positive experience and help with taking back some control. My diary gives an account of how I felt during my treatment and how I used my running and writing to give me a focus each day.

In the UK, one in seven females will be diagnosed with breast cancer in their lifetime. Breast cancer is the most common cancer in the UK, accounting for 15% of all new cancer cases (2016-18). There are approximately 150 new cases diagnosed every day. However, despite being the most common cancer, it is the fourth, not the first, most common cause of cancer deaths in the UK. This is because of an effective breast screening programme that allows for early detection and a much greater chance of survival. A recent study found that women who are diagnosed with early-stage breast cancer today are 66% less likely to die from the disease within five years of diagnosis than they were 20 years ago. In the 1990s, the average five-year risk of dying from breast cancer after being diagnosed with the disease in its early stages was one in seven. Today, it is one in 20.

Everyone's cancer journey is different. How you feel on day one will differ to how you feel after a month and after a year. When the treatment is over and you are, hopefully, 'cancer free' and everyone expects you to be back to normal, you may still feel that you will never be the same again. It will change your opinions about what is important, and you will reassess your priorities in life. The treatment affects everyone differently. I have heard many stories of how awful it can be. For me, it was certainly rough at times, and it was an emotional rollercoaster. However, despite the challenges of my cancer journey, I found strength through taking some control of what was happening to me, by putting on my trainers and going out for a run.

Chapter 1
Discovery and Surgery

Saturday 4th November 2017

'What's that?!' said Russ, my husband of only three months, as we lay dozing in bed on a wintry Saturday morning in November. I was lying on my left-hand side and Russ had his arm slung around me, his hand resting on my left breast. I felt down to where he had indicated. There was a hard lump, about the size of a grape, to the left of my nipple.

'I don't know,' I replied. I felt the equivalent position on my other breast. It felt very different. The lump was obvious to me, yet I had failed to notice it before now.

I wondered what I should do next. Feeling agitated and a little concerned, I got up and rang my doctor's surgery. I knew it was not going to be open, but the automated booking service allowed me to book ahead, and I arranged an appointment for just over a week's time.

I didn't know much about breast lumps or breast cancer, so I turned to the internet. Good or bad, Google is a resource of information. Firstly, I discovered that 80% of lumps found in women are most likely to be cysts. I took comfort in this, deciding that since this was the most likely scenario there was no reason to worry. I went out for my planned 10-mile run with a group of friends. I mentioned to Katie, my long-term running friend, what I had discovered. I was very matter of fact about it. There was no reason to be worried really, was there? It was most likely benign. But in the back of my mind was a little niggle. Should I wait for over a week for an appointment?

Chapter 1 – Discovery and Surgery

Should I treat this as an emergency? It didn't feel like one, but if it was something more sinister, shouldn't I get something done about it sooner? I really wasn't sure what to do. I didn't want to make a fuss if it was nothing.

I work at the Queen Alexandra Hospital in Portsmouth as a Medical Physicist, and my job involves carrying out safety and performance checks on X-ray equipment. This includes mammography equipment used for breast screening, which means I have a good relationship with the radiography staff in the breast screening unit. I rang up a senior colleague from this department and asked whether I should make an appointment sooner. She advised me that although it was most likely going to be nothing to worry about, it would be best to make an appointment sooner to alleviate the worry I was likely to experience whilst waiting to attend my appointment. I rang up the GP again, made an earlier appointment for two days' time and organised to take the necessary time off work.

Wednesday 8th November
I was examined by my doctor, who demonstrated to me the correct way to check my breasts. She asked whether the lump was painful (no) and filled out a standard referral form to the breast services centre. Going by the shape of the lump, she said it was most likely to be a cyst. I had no idea if this was honestly how she felt or whether it was just a reassurance tactic, but either way, it did help.

Friday 10th November
My referral appointment was booked in for 22nd November. Prior to this, I had already put myself forward to run a multi-day ultra event called the Druid's Challenge. This three-day event ran from 10th–12th November and covered the majority of The Ridgeway, starting from Ivanhoe Beacon, near Tring, and finishing near Swindon. The

Ridgeway is an Anglo-Saxon term given to an ancient track that runs along a high ridge of hills, and it's said to be Britain's oldest road. For over 5000 years, the route has been used by travellers, farmers and armies. It became a National Trail in 1972. The total distance for the Druid Challenge was 85 miles, covering approximately 29 miles, 27 miles and 28 miles over the three days. I had completed it in its entirety three years earlier, and partially over the previous two. This felt like a good way to measure how my long-distance training was progressing in preparation for my main focus in February 2018: a 100-mile race in Texas called the Rocky Raccoon 100.

As my GP seemed convinced all I had was a cyst, I was able to put it to the back of my mind completely and enjoy the event. Although much of the route merged into one long chalky track, I passed familiar places such as the villages of Goring and Streatley along the River Thames. This was also where, five months earlier, I'd started the Thames Ring 250. The checkpoints were a welcome site, providing an opportunity to replenish my food and fluids. On day three, I finally reached the welcome site of Barbury Castle Hill Fort, which reminded me that it was only a couple of miles to the finish and downhill all the way. I had managed to finish each of the three day runs faster than I had done three years previously, and I beat my overall time by an hour, becoming the winner in the over-50s category. This was evidence that my training was progressing perfectly, and that I was fit and well. Surely there couldn't be anything too seriously wrong with me, could there?

Wednesday 22nd November
I attended my referral appointment in mid-afternoon straight from work, which was easy enough since the department was only a couple of minutes' walk from my desk on a different floor of the hospital. Russ didn't come with me. As I wasn't worried, I didn't feel it necessary.

Chapter 1 – Discovery and Surgery

I was told to take a seat in a large, packed waiting room. There were women there of all ages, however, the majority were of a similar age to me, or older. Despite how busy it was, I didn't have to wait long before being called for my mammogram. Being 52, I'd had my first routine mammogram two years earlier, after being invited for one automatically at 50 as part of the breast screening programme's requirement for all women between the ages of 50 and 70 to be referred for one every three years. This had been reported as clear.

This time, the mammogram was carried out on both breasts just the same, but now I was being treated as a symptomatic patient. I am aware that many women feel anxious about this process as they worry about the mammogram being painful since the breast is compressed to make it easier to see the underlying tissue. However, the process is generally just a bit uncomfortable for a second or two. It's concerning that the false perception that it hurts puts many people off going for their breast screening. It's a quick, simple and standard examination carried out by experienced staff. Essentially, your breast is clamped still so that it doesn't move during the X-ray, and it just might save your life.

It was fewer than three years since my last mammogram, and as part of the standard breast screening programme in the UK, I would have been called up again the following year for my routine one. If I had developed anything in this time, it would be known as an interval cancer. What surprised me was that even though the lump was obvious to the touch, it was difficult to see on the images from the mammogram. I should have asked more questions at this stage, but as I failed to do so, it was some months later before I came to look at my images and discuss them further. I had expected the lump to be easier to see.

The next stage of my appointment was an ultrasound scan and biopsy. I knew this was a possible scenario for me as the information booklet I'd been given before my appointment explained the likely pathways depending on my results.

The doctor felt the lump and used the ultrasound probe to visualise it and then measure its size. I could now see the lump myself. The doctor then proceeded to feel under my armpit for my lymph nodes. She appeared to feel something there and used the probe again. From my viewpoint, it looked like there were lumps there too. Being completely unaware of what to expect from an ultrasound scan, this could simply have been normal lymph nodes, but I did not know. The doctor then attempted to take a sample of tissue from the breast lump, first numbing the area and then injecting some anaesthetic into it so that I wouldn't be in any pain. She spent even more time trying to get a sample from my lymph nodes, telling me it was important to get sufficient tissue for the results to be accurate.

I was beginning to realise that it was unlikely the lump was just a cyst, otherwise they would have simply drained it there and then. I felt calm but wanted to know if I had cancer or not. What else could it be? I tried to formulate a question in my head for the doctor that wasn't 'Do I have cancer?', because at this stage, I didn't expect they would have sufficient data to confirm anything. Instead, I asked what it could be if it wasn't a cyst. The answer the doctor gave me was vague and, as expected, she told me I'd have to wait for the results. Though she did not say the C-word, at this point, I suspected I did have cancer.

I then went back to the waiting area until I was called in to see the final consultant who would summarise what had happened and what would happen next.

Again, she didn't say I had cancer, but she told me the notes said the lump looked 'suspicious'. That certainly sounded suspicious to me! I was informed I would need to be booked in for an MRI scan since the mammogram did not show up the lump very well. They would need to scan both breasts to confirm there was nothing else present, and to ascertain the size of the lump more clearly.

I telephoned Russ and said, 'I don't think it's good news.' The biopsy results would be ready in a week, and I had been told to expect an appointment for the following Thursday afternoon after a meeting of the Multi-Disciplinary Team (MDT) in which surgeons, nurses, radiographers, radiologists, pathologists and oncologists come together to discuss results and agree a way forward.

Friday 24th November
As expected, my appointment date came through for the following Thursday. The seven-day wait was one of the worst times for Russ and me. Although I hadn't been told I had got breast cancer, it was looking likely. It was hard to sit idly by and just wait. As I already had a long run booked in with friends for the Sunday, I didn't even feel I could ease my anxiety with exercise. Sleeping was difficult. I started googling again. This probably wasn't a good idea, but throughout the process, I found that I coped much better when I had more knowledge and control of the situation. Knowing the worst that could happen, and the best, was important to me. Gaining this knowledge would also help me to ask the right questions at the right time.

I woke up somewhere between 2 am and 4 am. I tried going back to sleep but my mind was too busy with the mass of questions rushing around in my head. I had to get up and do something.

I googled Linda McCartney. What did she die of? Metastatic breast cancer. It may not have been the initial breast tumour that killed her, but the cancer spread to other vital internal organs and became much more difficult to manage.

What did Caron Keating die of? Breast Cancer. I knew this. I had read Gloria Hunniford's book on my way to Paris on the Eurotunnel, off to see the end of the 2006 Tour de France. Reading her account of losing her daughter to the disease had me in tears from the offset. I read the end of the book whilst sitting on a bridge over the Seine on the last day of my trip, and I cried again as the book came to its devastating conclusion.

Yet despite reading all this, I still hadn't become an avid checker of my breasts. Somehow, you just don't think it will happen to you.

I wasn't sure what I was searching for whilst googling into the early hours, it was just something to do. I looked up Kylie Minogue. She was still going strong. I looked up Olivia Newton John. She had been diagnosed with breast cancer in 1992 and was clear for a number of years. The cancer came back in her shoulder in 2013, and this year it had returned again, in her spine. She was currently in some pain and working on ways to manage it, but she was still alive 26 years on from her initial diagnosis.

When I came back from the appointment and had a little cry (and it was still only a little one!), Russ said, 'I don't know what I would do without you.' I knew how much he meant that, and it was important to me that he would be able to cope financially if I died. So, in the early hours when I could not sleep, I checked that everything was in place. All the paperwork was there. I could sleep in peace knowing that everything was sorted, and my family would be OK if something happened to me.

I also felt at peace through knowing I was happy. Instead of feeling that I had a lot to lose, I felt I'd had a good life and lived it fully. I was 52. There were many people who had much shorter lives than me, and I hadn't gone yet. I had time left, however long that turned out to be. I would take each day at a time and make the most of my wonderful, blessed life. I had achieved more in my running in the last few years, having run over a hundred marathons and having won the Liverpool to Leeds 130-mile canal race in 2016. Finally, after

Chapter 1 – Discovery and Surgery

completing the Thames Ring 250, I felt that, if I had to, I could now sit back and say, 'I did that'. I had also married the most amazing man and was part of a wonderful, extended family that I absolutely loved.

So, having confronted the worst-case scenario and sorted out everything in my power, I felt as ready as I could be for whatever might follow. What I found most difficult to cope with now was the not knowing, and the not being able to tell anyone. I had only mentioned the appointment to my running friends, Katie and Emma. We went out for a family meal vowing not to say anything. We didn't want to worry anyone until we had the full facts.

Sunday 26th November

The worry and tension spilled over on a 50k event in Kent that I was doing with a group of friends. It was called the Gatliff Marathon (despite being an ultra and not a marathon) and, while there was nothing preventing me from running, it felt as if an oppressive black cloud was hanging over me. We were meant to be doing the event as a team of four. I was the slowest of the group and knew that I would be running at my limit most of the time. The negativity hit me hard from the start. I tried to keep up, but the black cloud weighed on me. As waves of anguish and worry consumed me, I started experiencing breathing problems. What if this was my last long run? I wanted it to be an enjoyable one, but it was just too much for me to cope with. I needed to slow down and run without any additional pressure. I spoke to the only other woman in our group and explained that I had some negative stuff in my head that I was dealing with. She said she would stay with me while the other two ran ahead.

The pressure began to ease, and I enjoyed running at a more leisurely pace. From then on, I had a much better day and came home so much happier for having completed the event. Running is generally my mental medicine. On this occasion, it hadn't helped at first, but I had managed to find a way through the darkness and continue doing what I loved.

On the way home, I explained to everyone in the car what was happening. I wasn't upset and was quite matter of fact about it. I had come to terms with the possibility of having cancer, but the waiting and the secrecy was horrendous. I didn't want to worry anyone and have questions thrown at me that I didn't have the answers to, but it was impossible to pretend everything was perfectly fine whilst inside I was frantic with worry.

Thursday 30th November
My follow-up appointment for my biopsy results was in the afternoon, and this time I made sure I had Russ with me. We sat in the waiting room for about an hour before being called in. There were information screens within easy sight of where we were sitting that showed whose turn it was. Each time a new appointment number was displayed there would be a loud beep, and my stomach would lurch in anticipation. Russ felt the same. I looked at the others who were waiting, each with their own story to tell. There was a woman sitting opposite me with her partner. She looked how I felt. She was a similar age to me, and I had the feeling she was waiting for the same information. She went in before me and came out with a handful of leaflets. I could tell from the look on her face that the news hadn't been good. Her cancer journey was about to begin, and it would soon be my turn.

Coincidentally, a woman I knew from my running club came and sat next to me. She'd already undergone several operations from where her breast cancer had spread to other parts of her body. She acted like an old hand, smiling happily and talking about her experiences. I felt like I was just at the beginning of my journey. I was an inexperienced novice not knowing anything about the road ahead, and here was someone experienced who knew the ropes. I can't remember a great deal about what she said as I was nervous and preoccupied, but I found her positive attitude extremely encouraging.

My appointment number came up and my stomach lurched once again. Russ and I found our way to the treatment room. I was seen by a doctor that I had never seen before (and would never see again). She broke the news immediately that the lump contained cancer cells. She told me a little more about it. I had invasive lobular breast cancer. There are different grades of breast cancer: 1, 2 and 3. Grade 1 cells look mostly like normal cells and are usually slow growing. Grade 2 cells look less like normal cells and grow faster than Grade 1, and Grade 3 cells look completely different to normal cells and are the fastest growing. Mine was classified as Grade 2. The lymph node sample had come up negative, which was a good thing, but she said that the sample size was small, and she felt another biopsy was necessary to double check this.

Further tests had been carried out on the tissue sample. A hormone receptor test demonstrated that I was oestrogen receptor positive (ER+), progesterone positive (PR+) and HER2 (human epidermal growth factor receptor) negative. As cancer types go, I was told these results were good in terms of treatment. I could be given hormone therapy for several years after my treatment, and this would significantly reduce the chance of the cancer returning.

It felt like a huge amount of information to take in, but as I had been expecting to hear that I had cancer, I was not overwhelmed by the news. I noted down the information provided and listened to the next steps, some of which had been alluded to at my previous appointment. I would get appointments for an MRI (magnetic resonance imaging) scan to check both breasts and better define the current tumour. I would have a full body CT (computed tomography) scan to check whether there was evidence of spread to other sites of my body (staging), and I would have another biopsy. A follow-up appointment would be made with the breast surgeon once all the results were available.

I left the doctor and was seen immediately by a breast care nurse who ran through the diagnosis with us again and asked if we had any further questions.

'Will I lose my hair?' I asked. Perhaps it wasn't the most important issue to think about at this point, but since the nurse had mentioned chemotherapy was likely, it had been the first question I thought of.

'Yes,' she replied.

Despite all that was about to happen, the prospect of losing my hair was at the forefront of my mind. I have never been too bothered about having the most up-to-date hairstyle, but my hair grows very slowly, and I had managed to get it to a reasonable length for my wedding earlier in the year. If I lost all my hair, it would take absolutely ages to grow again. I also hated the thought of having people stare at me because I had a bald head.

The nurse gave me some leaflets to read at my leisure. I walked out through reception clutching them in my hand, lost in thought, just as I had seen the other women do earlier. However, I did feel more empowered. I had cancer. I knew what type I had and I knew I would be having surgery and probably chemotherapy and radiotherapy, though the order and extent of each would not be defined until the results of further tests.

Getting a diagnosis felt like a weight being lifted. I now knew what I was dealing with. Immediately after the appointment, I got changed into my sports gear and went for an energised run and a weights session at the gym. I could let family, close friends and work colleagues know what was happening and I could start taking back some control.

Chapter 1 – Discovery and Surgery

By the beginning of the following week, I had received the appointment dates for my MRI and CT scans. Working in the hospital had its advantages. The breast care nurse could easily ring me to sort out appointments and email me on my work email if she could not get hold of me.

I also had to make a booking with my GP to have my contraceptive coil removed. As it produced hormones, it was recommended that I get it taken out before treatment started.

It was stressful squeezing in appointments whilst continuing to work, but since I worked in the hospital it was easy for me to go straight from my desk to my hospital appointment and then continue with my job afterwards. From what I had already read, and based on the size of the tumour, I wasn't expecting the scans to find anything elsewhere, but this wasn't yet a certainty.

I now had to deal with telling people. Who should I tell first? I didn't want to throw it out to all and sundry via Facebook. I needed time to get used to the idea myself. It was hard breaking the news. I would always follow very quickly with the fact that the prognosis looked good so far. I had to deal with the look of shock and concern from other people and their reactions to it. I chose to only tell my immediate family, work colleagues and closest friends in the first instance, and I would deal with everyone else later, when I felt ready. I still found it hard to actually say to people that I had a tumour. For a number of weeks following the diagnosis, I used the term lump. The doctor had not called it a tumour, and somehow, I couldn't bring myself to call it one either.

After a few days' deliberation, I made the decision to cancel our 10-day trip to America for the Rocky Raccoon race. I could claim the money back on my insurance. We'd booked to visit the Space Centre at Houston, too, but although I'd been looking forward to it, we had no idea what would be happening or when. All I knew from the leaflets was that the treatment would be fairly prompt after diagnosis. I also pulled out of two 50-mile races that I had booked in for the following April and May. It wasn't certain that I'd be undergoing chemotherapy, but from talking to my breast care nurse it seemed quite likely, so I thought it best to plan for this possibility. I also had a preliminary entry for a 24-hour track race in Germany in June, which I would now be unable to attend. That was all my 2018 running plans decimated in one go! I wasn't as devasted as I had initially expected I would be. By making these decisions in advance I was regaining further control over what was happening to me.

We had also booked a trip to Paphos in Cyprus in early March; a much-anticipated family holiday. Russ's adult son Dan was coming with his partner Sarah and their two children, Evie and Frankie, as was his daughter Kirstie and her son Henry. My son John was also joining us, along with his partner Jess. Russ and I were doing the marathon and we had entered Dan, Kirstie, John and Jess into the 10k. While we ran, Sarah would look after our three grandchildren. Even if I couldn't go, I wanted everyone else to enjoy the break. I contacted the race organisers to change my marathon entry to the 10k. They were understandably sympathetic when they heard my reason for doing this and were happy to make the alteration.

As I was no longer taking part in the Rocky Raccoon, I scaled down my training a little. There was no point doing my planned 60-to-70-mile training weeks anymore, but I vowed to still do the races I had already entered up until the end of the year.

Wednesday 6th December
On the day of my MRI scan, I went into work as usual in the morning. My appointment notes advised that I could bring a CD of my choice to play during the procedure, as it can get very noisy. Some of my work

Chapter 1 – Discovery and Surgery

involved going into the CT (Computed Tomography) department, talking with radiographers, and carrying out safety and performance checks on the equipment, so I was very familiar with the area. The MRI scanner was next to the CT scanner and used the same waiting area, so I was familiar with the layout of the department. It was unsettling sitting in the waiting area as a patient in my dressing gown, rather than going straight into the CT control room to speak to staff.

I was called by a member of staff that I hadn't met before and taken to a changing room. Having previously had an MRI scan on my head, I was familiar with the set up and knew how noisy it can get. I was also aware that some people get claustrophobic, but as I knew what to expect, I felt confident I would be fine.

A radiologist I knew walked past whilst I was waiting to go in. She gave me a perfunctory smile but didn't stop. This was normal practice, but sitting there alone in my dressing gown, I felt very exposed and vulnerable.

I was brought into a side room, where a cannula (a small plastic tube) was fitted from where they would inject some contrast into my bloodstream. MRI contrast is a gadolinium-based liquid dye. The contrast works by highlighting specific parts of soft tissue. This would help to show up any tumours more clearly. Tissues that are being targeted will appear like they're glowing bright white, which makes them straightforward to detect and evaluate. MRI dye can help doctors detect tumours, identify if they are malignant or benign, and determine their growth stage.

The MRI scanner uses strong magnetic fields and radio waves to produce detailed images inside the body. The scanner is essentially a very deep, doughnut-shaped ring that contains powerful magnets. You lie on a long, narrow table, and the table is then moved so that the region of the body that needs to be scanned is positioned in the centre of the ring.

I was brought into the scanner room and asked to undo the top part of my dressing gown and lay forward on top of what looked like two plastic bowls, where my breasts would hang. It was a very undignified position to be in and, perhaps naively, not what I had expected. My head was positioned forwards on a headrest, and I was given a button to press if I experienced any problems during the scan. Because of my previous scan, I wasn't expecting to need to use it, but as I travelled, feet first into the ring and everything gradually got darker, I found myself feeling claustrophobic. This was made worse by the fact I could not see what was happening, as my head was facing down. When would I stop travelling into the ring? It seemed to go on and on. I hadn't expected to feel this way and I wondered how much worse it would be for someone who had no familiarity with how the equipment worked. Once I was in position, the radiographer spoke to me through the intercom to let me know they were ready to start. There were then a few different scans, which each took a few minutes to complete. Each one was accompanied by different noises as different scanning sequences controlled how the magnetic field turned on and off. I was listening to my chosen CD through the large earphones I'd been given, but it did not completely mask the noise.

Afterwards, I had my cannula removed and was guided back to the changing room. As it was a midday appointment, I wandered back to the office to finish my work for the day.

Wednesday 13th December
I had my second biopsy in the afternoon and went straight to the appointment from my desk. It was the same procedure as the previous one, only a little quicker this time. As I knew what to expect, it was also a lot less worrying.

Thursday 14th December
My appointment was booked for 4:30pm, but I was told to arrive an

hour early to drink some water, which would help improve the quality of the scan, which was to be a standard CT scan for staging cancer of the neck, thorax, abdomen and pelvis. I knew the radiographer, so we chatted a little beforehand.

This time, I was a lot more comfortable about the scan. I worked with this type of equipment and knew exactly how the machine operated. The CT scanner is also in the shape of a doughnut ring, but as it is not as thick as the MRI scanner, it feels less claustrophobic. The X-ray tube rotates around the body while the table travels through the ring, whereas during an MRI, the table remains stationary. Narrow beams of X-rays pass through the body while detectors opposite collect the radiation that has passed through it. The information is then transmitted to a computer. The CT computer uses sophisticated mathematical techniques to construct two-dimensional image slices of the body region that has been scanned. Each scan is carried out extremely quickly and is over in just a few seconds.

Sunday 17th December
I completed the Portsmouth Coastal Waterside Marathon, which is a pre-Christmas tradition. It was a relaxing, no pressure run, and I was joined by my friend Angie for a few miles along the course. As with many of my local friends, I got to know Angie because of my chosen sport. She is a little older than me and a member of another running club a few miles away, in Denmead. We met through a mutual running friend, Emma Louise. For many years, I had been regularly going to Queen Elizabeth Country Park to run around the hilly trails with Emma Louise, Angie and Len. We would typically run for about an hour. These were not ultra runs, but we had trained together in the past for the occasional marathon. Despite all that was going on, it was comforting to continue with my normal running routine.

For the following week, I continued with my normal daily work duties with no idea of when my operation would be. Based on the booklets I had read, the NHS had targets to meet, one of which stated that patients should have surgery within 31 days of consent. There were further targets for any follow-up chemotherapy and radiotherapy appointments.

I was not as anxious as I had been during my previous wait, as I did not expect for the cancer to have spread beyond the local area, but this was only an assumption based on the size of the tumour, what I had read and the difficulty of finding anything in the lymph nodes during my initial biopsy. This was just my layman's view and not based on much at all, so there was still a small nagging doubt in the back of my mind. It could have spread further; I would just have to wait and see. I would cross that bridge if and when I came to it.

Thursday 21st December

I took Russ with me to the appointment, along with a list of questions. Disappointingly, the surgeon explained that they had found evidence of cancerous cells in my lymph node sample from the second biopsy. The first ultrasound scan had indicated that some of the lymph nodes appeared abnormal, but the first biopsy sample size had been too small to reach any further conclusions.

Based on this result, I would need to have a full lymph node axillary clearance under my left arm. To do this, the surgeon would make a cut in my armpit to remove the lymph nodes. In some cases, not all the lymph nodes are removed, but the surgeon assured me that in my case, they would all be taken out. This would amount to somewhere between 20 and 30 lymph nodes. Once removed, they would be tested to determine how far the cancer had spread through them.

The MRI and CT scans had come out clear, which meant the cancer was confined to my breast region, which was fantastic news.

Chapter 1 – Discovery and Surgery

I was given the option of a mastectomy or removal of the tumour. With tumour removal, they would remove healthy tissue around the borders of the tumour and check that they had a clear margin free of cancer. If they did not get a cancer free border, they would operate a second time, which was likely to be a mastectomy. After discussions with the surgeon, I opted for just the tumour removal, as per his expert advice. I hoped this would be all that was needed in addition to the lymph node removal.

I signed the consent form for having surgery, which was described as a 'wide local excision'.

Looking at the staging system advice in my booklet, based on the tumour size and number of lymph nodes affected, I would be classified as having stage 3A cancer.

I was struggling to come to terms with how to deal with my work commitments. It was a very busy time, as someone was on maternity leave and another post was vacant. I was only going to make the situation worse, and this worried me intensely.

I asked the surgeon about how long I would need to be signed off for. He sat back in his chair, took a slow, deep breath and started to lecture me about putting myself first. He talked about his position as head of the surgeons' team and what would happen if he was not there. 'It's like a football team that loses a key player,' he said. 'They would struggle for a while and would have to adjust, but they would adapt, and they would manage. Work will still be there when you come back. Look after yourself first.'

This was the first of many lectures about putting myself first that I received throughout my treatment. I could sense Russ's eyes boring into me as I listened to the surgeon's advice; he was making sure that I was taking it all in. He knew how concerned I was about letting my work colleagues down.

I asked about chemotherapy. After having been told very early on that I would need it, the surgeon now said this was not definite. The news was a bit of a curveball, as based on what the first breast care nurse had said and what I had read, I'd been expecting to have it. This was a point when having Russ there was helpful. He later told me that what the surgeon had said was that it was likely but not definite. I didn't hear it the same way as he had, and I found the uncertainty disconcerting. It also meant it would be difficult to advise my work colleagues on what to expect after surgery.

In retrospect, perhaps the surgeon was trying to get me to concentrate solely on the surgery for the time being, as there was still the possibility of further operations afterwards. This was only the first stage of my journey, and there was enough to take in without being bogged down with the steps that might follow.

Having said all this, I still pressed the surgeon for an estimate of how much time I was likely to need off work following surgery, so I could give my boss a guide. He said two weeks. As I would not be permitted to lift anything heavy for up to six weeks after the operation, I would be limited to desk-based work for a while.

How long would it be until my operation? Christmas and New Year were imminent, and I knew this may affect when I was booked in. It could be within a month, but with the holidays coming, I guessed it might be longer.

Saturday 23rd December
I received a letter stating that my pre-operation assessment was booked for 28th December, less than a week away. It was also on the day when I was due to take part in a 45-mile event called the Winter Cross Ultra. Starting at Meonstoke, a small village about 20 minutes away from home, it's called the 'Cross' because of the shape of the

route. You start at the village hall then run out and back again in four different directions. I wouldn't have enough time to complete the 45-mile run before my pre-op assessment in the afternoon, but perhaps I could change to the shorter 50k option and fit that in. Hopefully, my elevated heart rate from just completing a 31-mile run would not cause too much of a problem!

Keeping an eye on my 86-year-old dad whilst having surgery and possibly chemotherapy presented another worry. About six years previously, Dad had moved from London to live near me in Portsmouth. I was very proud of him for taking on this large upheaval so late in life, and it meant that I visited him four to five times a week instead of four to five times a year. As his mobility had gradually deteriorated, he had become very reliant on me. My brother lived with his wife and three children in Germany and visited whenever he could, but as I lived less than half a mile away, it was easy for me to pop in regularly. I was happy to do so and involve him in my life where I could.

However, this was likely to change. He would not be able to rely on me so much, and I needed to find ways to make him more independent. He lived in sheltered housing, where he was looked after very well by the onsite staff, so he would be fine for a while without his regular trips out and visits. I needed to talk to him about it, but not today, which was one of our regular days out, and not while I was still taking in everything myself. Russ and I ran in the local country park with our friends while Dad did a crossword in the café until we returned. We then had coffee and cake together before taking him back to his sheltered housing in time for his 'Meals on Wheels' lunch.

Thursday 28th December
With one week to go until my surgery, I had to go in for my pre-op assessment. I also managed to run 50k at the Winter Cross Ultra event

in Meonstoke, which I thoroughly enjoyed. I then rushed back home to get showered and changed ready for my hospital appointment.

The assessment was straightforward. My blood pressure was taken, and I was weighed and asked various questions before being given some leaflets about how to prepare for the operation and reduce the risk of infection.

I was told that after my operation, I would have a drain attached to me to remove fluid from the wound. It would probably be in place for a week, and I would be shown how to empty it and measure how much fluid was being collected. I would have to come into hospital to get the drain removed later. Providing there were no complications, my operation was expected to be a day case. The surgeon would be carrying out a full axillary node clearance and removing the lump, together with some healthy tissue surrounding it, as we had previously discussed. If there was no cancer in the healthy tissue, no further surgery would be required. I had done my usual googling of what the operation entailed and found a cartoon-like representation of it. I don't think I could have watched a more realistic demonstration, which showcased all the blood and gore. All the lymph nodes would be removed in one mass. There was no searching for each separate node, as I had imagined in my head. It seemed less complicated, but the consent form came with a list of various risks, including numbness under the arm, lymphoedema and cording.

Lymphoedema is swelling that develops because of a build-up of fluid in the tissues in the body. The lymphatic system will normally drain the fluid away. By removing the lymph nodes from under my arm, my body would no longer be able to drain it as efficiently, resulting in an increased chance of swelling, particularly in the arm where the nodes had been removed. The surgeon had already mentioned the possibility of developing lymphoedema post-surgery, so I had already looked it up. Like everything else, the chance of

Chapter 1 – Discovery and Surgery

getting lymphoedema was a statistic and not a certainty, but there was a further risk post-radiotherapy. Once lymphoedema develops it cannot be reversed. However, you can reduce the risk by protecting your skin from cuts and grazes, insect bites and sunburn. Additionally, lymphatic drainage is improved by muscle activity and maintaining a healthy weight, which encouraged me to continue to exercise.

Axillary Web Syndrome (also known as cording) consists of rope or cord-like areas that develop beneath the skin just under the arm. While the exact cause isn't understood, it's possible that the trauma of the surgery leads to the scarring and hardening of the connective tissue surrounding the lymph vessels. These can restrict arm movement. It is not known why some people develop it while others do not. Treatment involves stretching, massage and exercises, which all help it to eventually clear up.

Saturday 30th December

Aware that my running days were about to temporarily come to an end, I squeezed in whatever events I could around the Christmas period. The Southsea Parkrun on 30th December, the 10k Pebble Dash along the beach at Southsea on New Year's Eve, and the New Year's Day Parkrun.

The Pebble Dash run is an annual fun event organised by a member of my running club over the festive period. It is not a race, and there is the option of doing a 5k walk or run or a 10k. Both start on Southsea beach and involve an out and back route entirely on the pebbly beach. It is exceptionally hard work. On this day, the wind was strong, and trying to move forwards against it was tough. Some chose to walk rather than run, while others switched to running along the promenade. It didn't really matter how you chose to run the event; it was just a bit of festive fun. A medal was presented to you when you finished – a pebble from the beach with a hole though it for the string so you could wear it around your neck. I was still tired after the Winter Cross and the previous day's Parkrun. The wind was relentless, but I couldn't bring myself to move onto the path away from the tough pebbly beach route. My time was running out. I'd be going in for my op soon, and this was one of my last chances to run. However long it took, I would work my lungs hard and stay on the beach. I felt I had to make the most of the time I had left.

Friday 5th January 2018
I arrived at the hospital at 7am for my surgery only to end up last on the list for the day. It was a very long wait, especially as I'd been nil by mouth from midnight the previous night. I tried not to feel anxious, but it wasn't easy. As the wait continued, I chatted to others who were also waiting, and then watched them go off for their operations. Even though most surgery goes without a hitch there is always the worry of being in the one operation that goes wrong. I feared the anaesthetic failing to work and being awake during the operation, and I feared not waking up again at the other side. I was also scared the procedure would leave me debilitated in some way. My logical mind kept saying, 'Stop worrying, everything will be fine,' but still I worried. It was a long, lonely wait, with far too much time to think.

Time then seemed to speed up as I was transferred to a waiting area near the theatres and taken to the operating room. All the staff got to work around me, and they were quick and efficient. I felt vulnerable, as I was completely in their hands. The anaesthetist explained what was going to happen and asked me some conversational questions. Not to get an answer, but to see me succumb to the anaesthetic. Then time stood still and there was nothing.

I woke up in recovery with Russ looking over me. Everything had gone well. Later, when I felt brave enough, I looked down at my breast and was surprised to find that it was still there. Despite all my

Chapter 1 – Discovery and Surgery

background reading and discussions with the surgeons, I really had no idea what to expect after the surgery, and I had no clue how they were going to go about removing the tumour. I hadn't even asked. No doubt this was partly because I had been too afraid to. The tumour had been removed through the same wide incision under my arm from where they had removed the lymph nodes. There was only one, four-inch scar under my arm, and my breast was fully intact. I had not expected this. It was a welcome sight and it made me feel more positive about getting through this first stage and moving on.

Chapter 2
Post Surgery and Pre Chemotherapy

Saturday 6th January 2018

Having been last on the list for surgery, I ended up staying in hospital overnight. It was now Saturday morning, and with fewer staff on weekend duty, I found it very difficult to get discharged. It took until late afternoon before I left the hospital. There was an advantage to this, however, as the doctor examined me and decided that I could have my drain removed before I left hospital. More good news! It was possible that I was feeling so positive because of all the drugs that were still coursing through me, but I was relieved to be going home at last, and with the freedom of not having the drain attached. That was the end of round one. Now it was time to recover and prepare for round two.

I walked the 10 minutes home from the hospital with Russ. I was so pleased to be on my feet again, even if my pace was a little slow and gingerly.

I had been told to wait at least two weeks before even thinking about running. The date was firmly etched on my mind, and in the meantime, I planned to walk as much as I could. The following day, I managed a 15-minute stroll to the local shops and back. I walked slowly, making sure that nothing felt uncomfortable near the wound site.

I rigidly carried out the arm and shoulder exercises I had been instructed to do, discovering that I had quite a lot of mobility in my arm at this point, although it was still early days. I was to do the exercises three times each day until my shoulder mobility was similar

Chapter 2 – Post Surgery and Pre Chemotherapy

to how it had been before the surgery, and then I was to continue the exercises once a day to help stop scar tissue from forming in my armpit or shoulder.

I was given some painkillers that were slightly stronger than over-the-counter ones, but I found that all I needed was a couple of paracetamols each day, and after three days, I did not feel the need for any further medication.

I walked daily, increasing from three miles on day one to five miles on days two and three. I then went up to eight miles.

Thursday 11th January

Throughout my diagnosis and treatment, I received so many messages of support. I'd been in hospital before for other reasons, but the depth of concern that came from my breast cancer diagnosis was unprecedented. At times, I found the attention overwhelming, but it was something I would have to learn to deal with. As part of my journey, I made several unexpected connections, and getting to know Ellen better was one of them.

In the early stages, I limited the number of people I talked to about the diagnosis because I was still struggling to deal with it myself. I didn't know how to respond when people asked, 'How are you feeling?' But Ellen had heard the news through a mutual friend, and she messaged me privately to let me know she was there for me. She offered to attend appointments with me, stressing that her work was flexible so she could do so. It was a genuine, unexpected offer that really touched me. She kept in contact throughout my diagnosis and then, post-surgery, she visited me after work.

Ellen is a legend to many, in ultra running circles, and I knew of her long before we met. I had seen her name down for a few ultra events, and when I entered the Thames Ring 250, I noticed that she had not only already completed it but had entered it again. It was a hard race to do once, let alone twice.

Today she had brought me a chocolate trophy with the words 'Screw Cancer' written decoratively on the front. It was an unexpected and thoughtful gift. I told her I would save it for when the ordeal was over, and I was out the other side. She couldn't believe I would be able to abstain from eating chocolate for that long. I checked the sell by date, which was May 2019, so I had plenty of time to eat it before it went off. We started discussing running, as you might expect from our mutual love of long-distance events. Ellen was planning her biggest challenge to date. The Monarch's Way nonstop race at the end of May. During this whopping 615-mile event, you were expected to average 43 miles every 24 hours for 14 days. The Monarch's Way approximates the escape route taken by King Charles II in 1651, after being defeated in the Battle of Worcester. It starts in Worcester and finishes in Shoreham by Sea.

We discussed when I might be able to do another ultra event. I decided that I would enter the Grand Union Canal Race (GUCR) the following year, in May 2019. This is a 145-mile race along the length of the Grand Union Canal, starting in Birmingham and finishing in London. Hopefully, I would have recovered sufficiently to begin training towards the end of the year. Russ was planning to take part in this year's event and hopefully I would be well enough to come and support him. I had cancelled most of my long runs for 2018 already, but I still had my entry for Autumn 100 in October. I very much doubted that I would be fit enough to complete this. The Autumn 100 event starts in the twinned villages of Goring and Streatley, where the Thames Path and Ridgeway cross. There are four legs to the event. Each leg is out and back, and you cover approximately 25 miles for each one. Legs one and four are along the Thames Path, while legs two and three are along the Ridgeway, in opposite directions. I decided I might be able to run 50 miles and complete the first two legs, so I left my entry in place just in case. Now I had the GUCR as a goal for further down the line, and I imagined eating my chocolate trophy at the end of it. Maybe that would be when I would finally get closure and be back to my old self again. I had no idea how my treatment would go, but based on what I had been told, I expected it to be over by the summer. Then I would need some time to recover and regain my fitness. The Grand Union Canal Race was 16 months away. This felt like a reasonable target to work towards and a fitting end to my journey back to health. Until then, the chocolate trophy would sit on the mantelpiece as a constant reminder of my future target, hopefully giving me the strength to keep going when things got tough.

Friday 12th January
A week after my surgery, I had an appointment to remove the dressing. I asked the nurse when I could start running again, hoping that perhaps it would be sooner than I'd previously been told, but she said to leave it two weeks as an absolute minimum. After that I should listen to my body and decide based on how I felt. It was possibly not the best advice for a long-distance runner used to ignoring their body signals and continuing to run even when everything hurts!

Saturday 13th January
Every Saturday is Parkrun day. I decided that whenever possible, I would do my local 5k event, even if I had to walk it. My friend Amy agreed to walk with me. Amy is the non-running partner of my ultra-running friend, Mich. I met Mich at our local Portsmouth running club many years ago and got to know him better when we both started training for ultra events. These longer races require running through the night, and for safety, it's helpful to have someone acting as a buddy runner. Mich and Russ were buddy runners for my first

100-mile race on the South Downs Way in 2013, and I had been a buddy runner for Mich on a couple of ultra events.

Amy and I started at the back and walked the entire Southsea Parkrun route along the seafront. I was wrapped up warm, and with Amy going at quite a pace, I had to work hard to keep up with her. We managed to complete the route in just under 50 minutes, and we weren't the last ones to finish. This is what's so special about Parkrun. It's a free event that's open to all ages and abilities. You will see children running with their parents, or another runner if the parents are no longer fast enough to keep up with their own offspring. There are people running with their dogs and there are friends running together and chatting as they go. Parkrun aims to cater for everyone.

Sunday 14th January
Today I walked approximately 15 miles around Portsmouth and Southsea while Russ ran. It poured with rain the whole time, so it wasn't the most enjoyable walk, but at least I was getting some fresh air. I was out for over four hours, which made me feel more normal, as this is something I am very used to doing at the weekends.

Thursday 18th January
As it was the second week after my operation, Russ and I met with the surgeon, who explained that the procedure had been a success and there was no need for further surgery. Only four of the lymph nodes had cancer in them, which was good news, but chemotherapy was now the recommended next step. The appointment was over quickly, and I was told to wait for an appointment from the consultant oncologist who would be responsible for arranging my chemotherapy treatment.

I continued to walk 10 miles a day. Amy and I did the Southsea Parkrun again. I could tell that my body was beginning to heal. However, my breast had doubled in size due to inflammation and swelling from where fluids, white blood cells and other chemicals had flooded the area to start the healing process. My shoulder mobility had got noticeably worse, and I had developed cording (Axillary Web Syndrome), but I was in no discomfort at all as I walked.

Sunday 21st January
I walked 10 miles along the South Downs Way while Russ ran. Aware that my two-week period of no running was now officially up, I occasionally ran a little in between walking. It didn't feel too bad, although I still felt a little tender.

Monday 22nd January
My little bit of running on the Downs made me realise that for now, it would be easier to run uphill, as there was less impact on my body. I decided that for my weekday running, I would start with some hill reps. I would walk downhill and run uphill to reduce the impact on my body. On my first run, I was out for an hour. I ran up the hill and walked down it again a total of 10 times. Although I took it slowly, I was able to get my heart rate up.

As the week progressed, the uphill running became less uncomfortable, though I quickly got tired of only going in one direction. I couldn't wait to go out for a normal run.

After my two weeks' recovery, I returned to work. It took a while to get back into a routine. I was also worried about the further disruptions to come.

Thursday 25th January
I attended a useful 'Demystifying Chemotherapy' course at the hospital's Macmillan Centre. They explained the side effects you might face during cancer treatment, and I asked about exercising through chemotherapy. I was told that the current recommendation

was to aim to get your heart rate up for 20 minutes three times a week. Going to the gym wasn't discouraged, but I was advised to use common sense when it came to hand washing and crowds.

They explained how chemotherapy treatment kills cancer cells by attacking the faster growing cells in your body. However, the drugs also kill off fast growing healthy cells. Chemotherapy is usually administered over the course of a few treatments that are typically around three weeks apart (but this depends on the type of chemotherapy and the type of cancer being treated). The time between treatments is called a cycle, and it's in this cycle that the cancer cells and healthy cells are destroyed. Some time is then given for your body to recover and replenish the healthy cells in time for the next treatment.

Cells in the mouth are usually replenished every three to five days. However, following chemotherapy there are no new cells available to replace the old ones, and this can lead to a dulling of the taste buds and a lack of appetite. You may also develop ulcers. The nurses recommended keeping a pint of salty water in the fridge to rinse your mouth out with. I would also be given some special mouthwash. Daily use would reduce the risk of developing a mouth infection.

Cells in the stomach are also affected, but this happens a little later in the cycle. We were given a list of foods to avoid and cooking advice for what we were allowed to eat. During chemotherapy, the stomach is less resistant to bugs. Unwashed vegetables, unpasteurised dairy and runny eggs were all to be avoided. Raw and undercooked foods could also make you sick while your immune system was busy fighting on other fronts, meaning fewer white blood cells were available to tackle harmful bacteria.

The platelets in the blood that help with blood clotting would also be affected, which meant it was important to avoid cuts, as it might be difficult to stop the bleeding.

Chapter 2 – Post Surgery and Pre Chemotherapy

Finally, and possibly most concerning, was the fact that white blood cells known as neutrophils would be affected around day seven to 10 in the cycle. Neutrophils are our body's best defence against infection, and at this point in the cycle, the body would be unable to fight off bugs. This meant it was extra important to use the special mouthwash to minimise any type of mouth infection. I was at risk of developing a serious condition called neutropenic sepsis, which would urgently require intravenous antibiotics. We were given action cards that listed the symptoms to watch out for and a 24-hour helpline to ring should we have any concerns.

I still didn't know whether I would lose my hair, as this side-effect was only discussed on a general basis. Some treatments would lead to hair loss while others would not.

We were introduced to the 'cold cap', a device that reduces the chance of losing your hair. It needed to be worn about 30 minutes prior to each chemotherapy treatment and for a further two hours afterwards. With treatments lasting hours already, this would likely mean being in hospital for most of the day. The cap would need to be kept at between -15 to -30°C and would need to fit tightly to every part of the scalp. Any areas with poor contact would still result in hair loss. This process would prevent the chemotherapy drug from damaging the hair follicles. However, it was not guaranteed to work. At this point, I was also told I would not be able to dye my hair. Since my hair was currently dyed blonde, I was not keen on the prospect of my natural brown appearing along with an unknown quantity of greys. I had been blonde for 10 years now – I had no idea how grey I actually was. I decided I would do without the cold cap. It sounded to me that even if I used it, my hair might still look awful and fall out anyway. To me, it did not seem worth enduring roughly five hours of freezing cold temperatures. I really did not like being cold. Each chemotherapy cycle was going to be uncomfortable enough, and I didn't want to add more layers to what already seemed to be a complex cycle of various side effects. The choice of wearing a cold cap is a very personal one. It makes the hospital stay longer, but many women find this a worthwhile trade off in return for maintaining their hair.

Sunday 27th January
Towards the end of 2017, I had decided to enter the Chilly Hilly 10k at Queen Elizabeth Country Park. This was where I often ran with friends and where I'd go for coffee and cake with my dad. I spoke to the race director and checked that I'd have enough time to walk the whole course if I needed to. I felt that continuing to enter local races, even if I walked them, would help keep me focused on getting back to my running.

As its name suggests, this is quite a hilly course, and I expected I would have to walk most of the downhills to protect my body from the impact. I knew the course would be very muddy, so I started at the back and walked from the start line. The mud and hills did make me question whether this was such a good idea so soon after my surgery, but once I was there, I thought I may as well take part, and I figured I could always walk the slippery bits. I found that I could happily run on the flats and downhills, and I would also run the uphill parts where I felt my fitness could cope. I was very careful on the downhills and clearly a little nervous, but I did manage to run the whole course, barring a few steep uphill patches. I became more confident as I progressed, and as the race thinned out and there was less chance of someone falling on top of me, it felt exhilarating to be back out on the trails that I loved. It had only been three weeks since the op and already I was running a muddy, hilly 10k race. This was something that I had not expected but had hoped might be possible. My breast was still swollen but it was not too uncomfortable. My arm mobility was still poor, and it would be a few weeks before I could lift any weights, but I was back running, and it felt great!

Chapter 2 – Post Surgery and Pre Chemotherapy

I continued to run a few miles most days in the week, ensuring I kept things steady. The following weekend was when I would have been going to America to run the Rocky Racoon 100, though I no longer felt disappointed. I had other things to focus on now – Autumn 100 in nine months' time and, if I couldn't manage that, I had the Grand Union Canal Race in my sights for May the following year. Since our plans had changed, we were now able to go to the British Spartathlon celebration evening in Hackney, where Russ could meet some of his running friends, many of whom were hoping to get into the Spartathlon ultra event later that year. Spartathlon involves climbing a mountain 100 miles into the course. If you take even a minute longer than the allotted 36 hours you're not considered to have finished the race. Russ had registered to run the race, and we were waiting to see if he would be successful in the ballot. Ever since we first travelled to Greece to support friends, Russ had wanted to be part of this iconic event, which covers 153 miles from Athens to Sparta and follows the footsteps of the Ancient Greek soldier, Pheidippides. Before the Battle of Marathon, he was sent by the generals of Athens to run to Sparta to ask for help to fight the Persians that had landed at Marathon. It is said he left Athens and arrived the next day, taking a day and a half to complete his journey. Hence, there is a strict 36-hour cut off. Checkpoints every five kilometres or so track the runners' progress, and a 'death bus' follows the course to pick up the runners who have fallen behind. In addition to the strict cut offs, runners must deal with the intense heat during the day and the cold of the mountains at night. All in all, it is considered one of the toughest ultra races there is.

While at the Spartathlon evening, an ultra-running friend asked me if I had entered, to which I laughed out loud. The qualifying criteria to even enter this race were out of my league. I had been out to Greece to follow the race five times now. I'd watch the participants run through the streets of Athens before moving onto the quieter roads that skirted the coast. The runners would try to keep their core temperature down by dipping their hats into cool water and stuffing ice in buffs, which they then wore around their necks. They invariably looked hot and exhausted by the time they reached Ancient Corinth, 58 miles in. These runners were at the top of their game, and even they were finding it tough. Over 40% of participants are not expected to finish, so I was certain I was not good enough to do this race, though I was happy to stand out in the gorgeous sunshine and support our UK runners, many of whom had become friends over the years of us attending the event.

Despite much of the race being on dusty roads and not particularly scenic, entrants come from all over the globe to participate, so it is always oversubscribed. This means it's very difficult to get into unless your running speed is enough to guarantee you an automatic qualification, which only the most elite ultra runners can reach. You must meet certain criteria even to enter the ballot. The previous year, Russ had managed to achieve the 100-mile qualifying time at a 24-hour track event at Tooting Bec, London. After registering for the race in January, he now had to wait until the end of March to find out if he'd been successful. The race was at the end of September, so it was likely that I would be through my treatment by then and would be able to support him in Greece.

My experiences with cancer would later cause me to reconsider my decision to only attend Spartathlon as a supporter. Life-changing experiences can change your perspective and make you re-evaluate your plans and the paths you take.

Thursday 8th February
Today I had my first appointment with the consultant oncologist in relation to my chemotherapy treatment.

Chapter 2 – Post Surgery and Pre Chemotherapy

I queued up in the main reception of the Oncology Department to show them my appointment letter. I was given a reference number and asked to sit down. This was my first time in this particular waiting area, but all my appointments from now on would take place here. Within five minutes, my number came up and the monitor indicated a sub-waiting area for me to transfer to. This was much smaller, and all the people present were waiting to see the same consultant. This time, I hadn't brought Russ with me, but I began to wish that I had. The people around me were clearly further on in their treatment. I felt very insecure and inexperienced. A lady in her mid-thirties arrived. She was completely bald and wearing large, gold hoop earrings. She looked exceptionally confident, and I felt envious of her outward self-assuredness. Perhaps, further down the line, I would feel as confident as this young woman, but right now, I was sitting there alone and feeling apprehensive over what would happen next.

First, I was called to be weighed and have my height measured. I knew from my 'Demystifying Chemotherapy' course that this was how they would determine how much of the chemotherapy drug to give me. I then had quite a lengthy wait to be seen by the oncologist. It was something I was already getting used to, and I knew it was something you had to accept while being treated in a busy NHS hospital.

When I finally met with my consultant, she gave me a number of sheets listing the many side effects that were possible, but not definite, for my specific drug cocktail. Knowing I wouldn't have time to read it all in detail, I put the paperwork down to look at later and concentrated on what she was saying. I asked about doing exercise and she encouraged me to do as much as I could of what I would normally complete. I decided not to mention that my routine involved running 40 to 50 miles on some weekends and running a total of five to six times per week.

My treatment is called FEC-T, which is standard for my type of breast cancer. I would be having six cycles of chemotherapy, with each cycle lasting three weeks. The first three would be FEC. This is named after the initial of the drugs used, namely F – fluorouracil; E – epirubicin; and C – cyclophosphamide. For the second three cycles, I would be given the drug Docetaxel (also known as Taxotere).

The list of side effects was quite extensive and significant. Some were similar for all cycles, whereas some were specific to the docetaxel – when I was on this I would then worry about the joint pain, numb feet and hands, and changes to my nails.

At this point, I was also told that I would lose my hair, and that the hair loss would probably begin at the end of the first cycle. It was helpful to finally have this confirmed. I was referred to have an NHS wig fitting at the hospital's Macmillan Cancer Centre.

My first chemotherapy appointment had been booked for 21st February, despite me asking the breast care nurse if it could be arranged for after my trip to Paphos in Cyprus. This was meant to be our big family holiday, which included our children and their partners and our three grandchildren. Russ was going to be running a marathon and I had my name down for a 10k. I was really hoping that Russ and I would be able to join everyone. My consultant kindly moved my first treatment back three weeks, which would give me time to go on holiday and then sort out all my outstanding work commitments before starting chemotherapy.

Sunday 11th February
I ran the Punchbowl 20 with my friend Iaan. I met Iaan through my local running club. We had a mutual interest in doing ultras and often ran together on club nights with a group of like-minded people. Iaan had run a few 50-mile ultras and had been one of the runners on a 100k team event alongside me, Russ and our friend, Mich. He

is over six-foot tall, and his long stride means that he can walk very fast, which is a real advantage in ultra events. The Punchbowl 20 was another of the races I had entered before my surgery in the hope that I might have recovered enough to do it. It was organised by the Long Distance Walkers Association (LDWA) and as a result there were usually more walkers than runners taking part. The event was not really a 'race' but a day out along the trails around the Devil's Punch Bowl in Hindhead, Surrey. You were provided with some course notes to help get you round, with an occasional checkpoint stop for food and drink. It would have been perfectly acceptable for me to walk the entire event. However, on the day, I found that I was fine to run most of the route, and Iaan and I had a lovely day jogging through the Hampshire countryside.

Friday 16th February
I met with my GP to discuss how and when to take time off work, and she recommended I take the first four weeks off sick so that I could see how I coped with the first cycle and get through the first week of the second one. From that point on, depending on how I felt, she recommended that I look at the possibility of working from home. Work was still as busy as ever, but I also had the added stress of various visits to the doctors, occupational health and a wig specialist. Fortunately, most of these were at the hospital where I worked, which made everything easier to cope with.

Friday 23rd February
I had my initial consultation with Rachel, the wig specialist, and I brought Russ and my grandson, Henry, along. As Russ and I were both off work on Fridays, we were able to take care of Henry while our daughter, Kirstie, was at work. During the appointment, I tried on a number of wigs. Rachel had long dark hair with red highlights. She revealed during the session that she had alopecia. She said she

had over 40 different wigs at home to choose from. She was the perfect person to be empathetic towards the needs of someone who was shortly going to be experiencing hair loss themselves, although I was mindful that mine would be temporary. Rachel was at least 20 years younger than me, and she had to deal with this for a lifetime. However, she had a fantastically positive attitude, which certainly helped me to put my situation into perspective. Ultimately, it was quite a fun experience, especially with Henry in tow. I chose a wig that I liked, and Rachel ordered it in my size. There would be a chance for me to try it on when it arrived.

As well as the hair loss, I was likely to lose my eyebrows and eyelashes. Rachel gave me the leaflet of a person who would be able to tattoo my eyebrows on through a process called microblading.

Back at home, I looked up the website and read about the types of treatments on offer. They included tattooing nipples on women who had undergone breast reconstruction. The website also mentioned that the owner had been badly burned in her youth and, therefore, had personal experience of having this kind of treatment. Again, I knew she would have empathy towards my own circumstances.

I rang up to ask about the procedure and was told that ideally, to get the best results, I would need two sessions before my chemotherapy started. I would possibly need a further top up while my eyebrows were growing back, but after that I would not need to do it again (although I believe there are many people who have this type of treatment regularly because they like the effect). It cost more money than I would normally be willing to spend, but this was important to me. Again, it felt like I was taking control of the situation, and that helped me to cope better.

Saturday 24th February
I arranged for my husband's niece to cut and dye my hair. I went from

Chapter 2 – Post Surgery and Pre Chemotherapy

having long blonde hair to a short brown style. This was a big change, but I felt that returning to my natural colour and going to work with my new style would make the transition to losing my hair less of a shock, to both myself and others. My hair would also grow back brown, and as I wouldn't be able to dye it for six months, I figured I may as well get used to being a brunette again. I felt uncomfortable coming into work with a new hairstyle, as it was so different to my previous look and brought lots of attention my way. But it only took a day or two for everyone to get used to it and for the comments to stop. It meant that I also got the odd question about my drastic change from colleagues with whom I did not work closely. However, as the news of my health was beginning to spread, I felt ready to tell them, 'I've got breast cancer.' I saw how uncomfortable that was for them to hear, so I would quickly follow up with how they had caught it early and the prognosis was good. For me at least, it was beginning to get easier to talk about.

Sunday 25th February

I ran the New Forest Trail Marathon with Iaan. As we'd suspected, we did get a little lost, as there were no signs en route or any marshals to direct you at significant turns in the event. We had some maps to follow, but due to our inexperience with this type of event we made some navigational mistakes. Despite this, the weather held out for us, and we had a gorgeous day out while trying to work out where we were and where we were trying to get to. It was a great way to forget about what was to come and a fitting last marathon for a while. The next one I expected to run was the Portsmouth Coastal Marathon at the end of the year. At least, that was my current plan.

Wednesday 28th February

I managed to squeeze in my first eyebrow tattoo treatment just before my holiday to Cyprus. The treatment involves light scratching of the skin along the eyebrow line. In this way, fine strokes of ink are carefully applied into the upper layers of the skin so that it looks like your natural eyebrow hair. Apparently, still having my eyebrows in place made it easier to follow my natural eyebrow line. Before the microblading began, an anaesthetic was applied to the area. Although not painful, the process was a little uncomfortable and brought on an uncontrollable urge to sneeze. When first applied, the treatment produced very dark, thick eyebrows, and initially I did not feel comfortable with the result. However, I was told that the look would soften over the next few days, which it did. In the end, I was happy with it.

The post-treatment phase involved applying special creams and gels to my eyebrows to stop them drying out and to prevent infection, which is why it couldn't be done once the course of chemotherapy had started. My second appointment was booked for 9th March, following my return from Cyprus. Since this was only five days before my first chemotherapy treatment, I ran it by my chemotherapy consultant. She reassured me there would be sufficient time for my skin to heal before my first treatment.

In these early stages before my treatment began there was a lot to take in, and at times it felt overwhelming. I tried to cope and keep in control, but as it got closer to our holiday and there was a chance we might get snowed in at home, I became more distressed. I really needed to get away for a few days and forget about everything that was happening to me.

Friday 2nd March

As our flight was early in the morning, we decided to drive to the airport late evening the night before. Due to all the bad weather warnings, we were worried about how long the journey would take. The snow had settled locally, but as we travelled closer to Gatwick, it gradually disappeared. It looked like we were actually going to make our holiday after all!

Sunday 4th March
The holiday was fabulous. Russ completed his marathon, and I was able to cheer him on at the end after finishing my own 10k.

I gave the run my best shot even though 10k is not really my distance. I was chuffed to come second in my age group and be awarded with a trophy. It was a wonderful way to finish off my running before starting chemo.

The rest of the family followed on after me, and I was able to cheer each of them on. They clearly didn't find it easy. Our children do not possess our love of running, but it was great to have them share in what we do and to see them taking pictures of each other proudly wearing their medals while talking about what they would do the next time they took part in a race.

Wednesday 7th March
I returned to work early to have my first pre-chemotherapy blood test. The next few days were busy with handover meetings with colleagues and tidying up my desk. This was interspersed with appointments to pick up my wig and get my final eyebrow treatment. There seemed to be such a lot to do, and I could feel my stress levels building alongside the worry over what was to come.

Thursday 8th March
The lottery for Spartathlon took place this evening and, against all the odds, Russ's name came up! Suddenly, his dream had become a reality, and he would be running in the iconic event at the end of September. This was something he had been dreaming of for years. Between now and then, he would need to lose a stone in weight and focus hard on his training. I hoped my cancer treatment wouldn't

distract him too much. The next few months were going to be difficult for us. Hopefully, my treatment would be over by late September, and I would be able to go to Greece with him. I had already agreed the leave with work so that I could go if I was well enough. But right now, it seemed such a long way away and I had a lot to get through before then.

Saturday 10th March
With my first chemotherapy treatment due to start the following week, I decided to run the Southsea Parkrun for what might possibly be the last time for a while. I privately hoped that I could keep doing Parkrun throughout my treatment, but that was not a certainty. As I felt fit and well, I decided to start near the front and run at pace. I finished with my fastest time for a few years. This felt like a good end to my current 'normal' life. I had recovered well from the surgery just over two months ago and felt as fit as I could possibly be in the run up to the chemo.

Sunday 11th March
I took my dad for possibly his last weekend outing for a while to the Queen Elizabeth Country Park. His poor mobility prevented him from getting out on his own. I wasn't sure whether I would be able to continue with these trips, as I would need to minimise my risk of catching anything by staying away from public spaces as much as possible. I knew it would be OK to run outside in the fresh air, but sitting in a busy café afterwards would not be such a good idea. As well as spending time with Dad, I had an enjoyable run along the South Downs Way, which is one of my favourite places to run. I wondered to myself, *When will I be able to run here again?* These last few runs were so very precious. The unchartered waters that lay ahead felt alien to me, and I felt daunted and scared.

Chapter 2 – Post Surgery and Pre Chemotherapy

Monday 12th March
I met with my chemotherapy oncologist. Unsurprisingly, my blood results were fine, and I was fit and well and ready to begin my first chemotherapy treatment on the Wednesday afternoon as planned. There was nothing more to be said at this meeting. The treatment process had been explained, so it was just a case of getting on with it and seeing how I responded.

In the evening, I went to the gym and met with my instructor. For the duration of my treatment, I had booked one session a week with him, but it had been agreed that I could cancel if I didn't feel up to it. We would take each week as it came and do a gym session if I felt able. I booked the sessions for the quietest times at the gym, when there would be less people around, and I planned to come armed with antibacterial wipes and hand gel to ward off any germs.

Tuesday 13th March
The day before my first treatment, I managed a run along Portsdown Hill from the back of my house. It's a 5-mile route out and back along the ridge overlooking Portsmouth. As I got to the turnaround point, I stopped to take a breath and admire the view. Unexpectedly, I started to cry. Suddenly, it all seemed so very real and completely overwhelming. I had spent so long getting organised for what was to come and maintaining as much control as I could. But now I was going into the unknown, and I sobbed loudly for the fear of what was to come and for all the changes that were about to take place. The tears did not last long, but it was the first time I had really wept. Perhaps I needed the release. I was letting it all out to prepare for the next significant chapter of my life. I sat for a short while on the grass and looked across Portsmouth. It was an amazing view and I felt so lucky to be alive and to be able to witness it. I calmed myself down and regained my composure for the run back home. I'd had my cry

Chapter 3
Cycle 1

Wednesday 14th March

The day of my first chemotherapy dose had arrived. This was the last time I was going to feel completely well for some time, and despite having only just run the previous day, I decided to squeeze in a 10-mile run before the appointment. I couldn't see what harm it would do. It was a route that I ran regularly during training. It started with a hill and then passed through some fields near a golf course, taking me behind the fort where Russ and I had our wedding reception. The final few miles were along the foreshore next to the Farlington Marshes Nature Reserve, which is part of the Portsmouth Coastal Waterside Marathon route. The majority of the last five miles were completely flat, with lovely sea views.

I did not feel the need to cry this time. I just wanted to get on with my treatment.

My appointment was at 1:30pm. Russ had taken the day off work so he could attend my entire first session with me. We went to the same main reception area in oncology, but this time our waiting area was in a little corner separate from the radiotherapy patients.

I was given two wristbands to wear. One was the typical hospital band with my name, date of birth and hospital number, and the other was bright red to signify that I was allergic to something (in my case aspirin). For me, wearing the wristbands signified I was now a patient with a condition rather than just someone coming in for a quick appointment. After half an hour, a group of us were called into the main chemotherapy clinic where the treatment was

Chapter 3 – Cycle 1

to be administered. I was directed to a specific chair that had been assigned to me for the afternoon. I explained to the nurse that I had decided not to wear a cold cap and that I did not want a PICC line either. A Peripherally Inserted Central Catheter, or PICC, is a line that goes into a vein in your arm. The procedure is carried out under local anaesthetic and the line can remain in situ for many weeks and makes administering the chemotherapy drugs more straightforward. I had not been given any advice previously about the pros and cons of a PICC, but I was aware that having one would give me an added infection risk, so I would have to come into hospital more often to have it checked and cleaned. Having this visible on my arm would also be a constant reminder that I was still a patient, and once I had left the hospital, I wanted to feel as far removed from that as I possibly could.

My nurse, Caroline, introduced herself to me. She had her own trolley with her name on it and everything she would need for administering each of the chemotherapy drugs. She gave me some steroids to take and an anti-sickness tablet. She then took my blood pressure, pulse and temperature and noted down the results.

Three different nurses were working alongside each other, all treating many patients at the same time. As soon as someone got up to go home, someone new would immediately replace them. The people present were all at different stages of their treatment. Some, like me, were just beginning their journey, while others were on their last session.

As an FEC patient, my first drug was epirubicin. First, the nurse fitted a cannula to my right arm near my wrist and flushed it through with saline. The epirubicin drug comprised a total of 160mg spread out over three huge syringes full of bright red liquid. Caroline injected these by hand through the cannula, keeping a constant eye on me throughout to ensure I didn't have an adverse reaction. The other two drugs, fluorouracil and cyclophosphamide, were administered electronically by machine, and Caroline then left me to go and tend to someone else. In between each drug, there was a 10-minute flush of saline solution. As each solution finished, the machine would beep to let the nurses know that a person needed further attention. The nurses were kept extremely busy. They had an ongoing supply of patients coming through the department all day until 8pm.

I was presented with a bag of drugs to take home, and I struggled to absorb all the instructions that came with them. I was given steroids and some anti-sickness tablets to take before meals for the next three days, along with some mouthwash. I wrote on the boxes the days that I needed to take the tablets so I wouldn't forget. The steroids were meant to help counteract some of the initial side effects of the chemotherapy. In addition, I was given a box of five pre-filled filgrastim syringes and instructed to inject them into my abdomen from day five on. These syringes contained something called Accofil, which is used to help your body make more white blood cells to combat the loss of neutrophils at about seven to 10 days post treatment. The aim is to prevent neutropenia (when your neutrophil count is low, and you are at higher risk of infection). I was instructed to store them in the fridge and only take them out when I needed them.

During the treatment, I wheeled my drug cart to the ladies' so I could go to the toilet. It continued to administer the chemotherapy drug while I went. My urine was bright red, the same colour as the epirubicin. Even though I had been warned about this, it was still quite a shock to see the bright red colour in the toilet, which indicated that some of the medication had already passed through me. I was told it should only be like this for a day.

At the end of the session, I was given a list of dates and times for all my further treatments and told that I would have an appointment with my consultant a couple of days prior to each one. The treatments were always on a Wednesday, exactly three weeks apart. When I got home, I put all the medicine neatly in a box on the kitchen side so that I would know exactly what I had, and I didn't forget to take any of it. I also put my chemotherapy booklet there. This was where the nurse had recorded my blood levels from my recent blood test and would continue to do so for the following five cycles after this one. I ripped the hospital labels from my wrist. I was no longer a patient and did not want to feel like one anymore. I was just me again. I talked good humouredly to Russ in the evening and tried to act as though nothing untoward had happened. My relaxed attitude helped Russ to cope with what was going on. I did not want him to worry about me.

In bed that night, I found myself lying on my back, wide awake, waiting for something to happen. I didn't know what, but I knew I had this poison running through my body. While it was attacking my cancer cells, it was also destroying my healthy cells. I had been warned of some of the side effects I was likely to experience, but I didn't know how I was meant to feel right now. I had heard of people feeling nauseous straight after their treatment, but so far, I felt OK.

Thursday 15th March
The following morning, I got up at 3am. I knew it was the steroids making it difficult for me to sleep. The day before, I had been given my first 8mg dose of dexamethasone just past the recommended cut-off time of 2pm.

I felt a little fragile but otherwise OK, so I decided to make some hot ginger tea to help my stomach settle. I would take an anti-sickness tablet and then try to eat something close to my normal breakfast time. I also decided to be proactive and start using the special mouthwash I'd been given, both in the morning and at night.

I spent the morning waiting for something to happen, but generally, I still felt OK. My stomach was a little unsettled so I did not feel like eating very much, but I couldn't say that I was nauseous.

After Russ left for work, I went for a run across the fields at the back of our house. It was the same route I had done earlier in the week when I had sat down and cried. I felt fine and was grateful that I was still able to run, which wasn't something I had expected. The anti-sickness tablets were obviously working for me. The nurse told me there was no reason for anyone to feel sick after chemotherapy. If you still felt nauseous while taking the prescribed anti-sickness pills, they would try and find you an alternative that would work better for you.

Over the next couple of days, I found myself struggling to get to sleep at night. In the early days of my treatment cycle, it was mainly the insomnia that affected me.

Saturday 17th March
As I had promised myself I would, I did the Southsea Parkrun. Despite the cold and threat of snow, I took it steady and was able to run comfortably. However, I was aware that I was not feeling 100 percent. My head was a little hot and I felt a bit stuffy, like you do at the beginning of a cold, but it was nothing too serious.

That night, I became aware of how dry my mouth felt, and I was incredibly dehydrated. I wondered if this was from using the mouthwash before I really needed it. It didn't seem like I was producing saliva, and the skin inside my mouth felt crinkly, similar to how your feet and hands get after lying in the bath for too long.

Sunday 18th March
Four days had passed since the start of my treatment, and it was time to start self-administering my filgrastim injections. I read the instructions from cover to cover and decided I was going to do this without any help from Russ. I felt I needed to be on my own. I wasn't looking forward to it at all. I had to use the antiseptic wipe provided

to clean the injection site somewhere on my abdomen and then pinch the skin prior to injecting. I had sufficient fat around my abdomen to pinch. There seemed to be more than usual. This was probably due to the water retention that came with taking steroids. I figured it would settle itself down in a few days once I stopped taking them. It was a thinner needle than for a blood test so I told myself I wouldn't feel it so much. I managed to push the needle in but could only press on the plunger slowly, which made the whole process more drawn out. It wasn't hard to do but I hated it. I also worried about forgetting to do it, which was something I would continue to fret over until all the injections were done. I still had four more to go.

Russ and I had entered a 10-mile run in the New Forest. However, the weather was bitterly cold, with snow on the ground and a biting wind. We decided not to travel to the event and instead do my regular 10-mile route together. We ran in the opposite direction from usual, which, in retrospect, probably wasn't such a good idea, as for the first four miles we were fighting against the wind. My legs did not want to run. The chemotherapy drugs were beginning to take their toll. I couldn't pinpoint what was wrong, but after running only a mile it felt like I had been going for a full 10. I had my buff pulled up over my face to protect me from the worst of the biting wind and, not wanting to spoil Russ's run, I plodded slowly on without complaining. Unfortunately, Russ wasn't feeling great either. He resisted moaning through guilt. How could he complain when I was still running despite what I was going through? It was a difficult run for both of us. We got there in the end, but I would mark this day as one to remember in terms of when in the treatment cycle the chemotherapy drugs made it more difficult for me to exercise. Russ and I were just glad we hadn't headed off to the New Forest. At least when we had finished our awful runs we were straight back home for a nice warm bath.

Monday 19th March

I had stopped taking the steroids, but sleep continued to elude me. I got up around 3am and pottered around the house after having a ginger tea to settle my stomach. I emptied the dishwasher, sorted out some clothes for washing, went on the computer for a while and did some puzzles. I did a little work, too, but I found it hard to concentrate on anything for long.

Tuesday 20th March 2019

Even though it took a while to get out the door, I went for a 5-mile run. I was sluggish and knew I wasn't right, but I still managed to run the whole way and felt better afterwards for having done it. My mouth felt awful, but I told myself this didn't affect my legs!

I met a friend for a catch-up and found that I no longer liked the taste of my usual coffee, so I had some fizzy water instead. Apart from this I felt relatively normal. In the morning, my temperature had felt a little high and I had taken a couple of paracetamols, but throughout the rest of the day I didn't feel the need to take any more.

The following day, I was booked in at the gym. I didn't really feel like going, but I forced myself to attend. I went on the rowing machine for a warmup and found it difficult to put in any effort. I was just going through the motions. For my gym session, I only used light weights and we spent more time chatting than doing any activity.

To add to this, I had a really heavy period. Most recently, my blood loss had been light and infrequent. To have a heavy period now was totally unexpected, and I was concerned because my red blood cells were already going to be affected by the chemotherapy. I had chatted this over with my consultant and we had decided that I should go on iron tablets, which was the only supplement I would be taking for the duration of my treatment.

Despite how I was feeling, I managed to run on Wednesday evening and again on Thursday morning. These were gentle outings, but I was pleased to be able to run for the entire time. I was relieved to find that I wasn't feeling as bad as I had done earlier in the week. Perhaps I was over the worst of the first cycle.

A half marathon event was being held at the Queen Elizabeth Country Park on Sunday, and I decided to contact the organisers, whom I know well, to see if I could enter on the day. Based on my previous efforts, I thought I could just about run a half marathon distance if I walked the hills. It was covering similar routes to the Chilly Hilly I had done in February, and I would know all the marshals, which meant that if I had any issues, I could stop at one of the water stations.

Sunday 25th March
When I arrived at the park for the half marathon, I saw quite a few people I knew, and I had to make it clear as they approached that I wouldn't be hugging them. Although I was able to run, I was at a point in my chemotherapy cycle where my infection risk was high, so that kind of close contact felt like an unnecessary risk.

My friend Angie, who I did regular weekend trail runs with, was taking part too. We're roughly the same when it comes to running ability, although, 11 days since my first chemotherapy treatment, I had no idea how I would cope with a half marathon distance.

I progressed happily at my steady pace, but when I came to a steep hill (and there are a lot of them on the local trails here), I decided to use my usual strategy, which was to run slowly as far as I could and then, if I had to walk, alternate between walking and running a few steps, until I reached the top of the hill.

About six or seven miles in, I caught Angie up, and we ran together, encouraging each other along. We ran side by side until we had about a mile to go. At this point, I suddenly found that I was able to push ahead. I came first in my age group, which was a lovely surprise, and the race organiser was really chuffed for me and became quite emotional as I received my prize. So far, the chemotherapy wasn't taking away what I loved to do.

Monday 26th March
My pre-chemo appointment was a week earlier than it normally would be so they could assess how I was coping so far. I was upbeat when I saw the nurse. I told her I was feeling much better than I had expected to feel. My mouth had not been great, but I was back to eating normally, and I hadn't lost my sense of taste.

'That will get worse,' she said.

She asked about my energy levels, and I proudly told her that I had managed to run a half marathon the day before.

'That will get worse,' she added.

Her lack of positivity was disappointing, but I decided to keep doing what I was doing until I could no longer manage it. I would walk when I couldn't run. That was my plan, and I would stick to it for as long as I could.

The nurse told me that between now and my next chemotherapy treatment in a week's time, I would continue to feel better. This was fantastic news, as it meant I could start planning my work from home schedule and manage some day-to-day tasks. I would also be able to visit my dad.

At my first chemotherapy session, the loss of my hair was a long way from my thoughts. I had decided that I would take things a day at a time, focusing only on what I needed to deal with as different symptoms arose. I was now beginning to feel better. As my symptoms waned, my thoughts went back to my hair. I had already ordered some scarves. I began reading up on hair loss again. I asked the nurse when

Chapter 3 – Cycle 1

I might start to lose it. She said I was likely to start experiencing hair thinning after approximately two weeks and that I would lose it all early in the second cycle. This meant it would start falling out in a couple of days' time. The most common timescale I read was 14–16 days after the first cycle. It also said I would feel some tenderness in my scalp. I had not expected that. I had previously seen some frequently asked questions where someone had asked, 'Did it hurt?', but I had just glossed over it. Somehow, I had thought, *What an absurd question. Why ever would it hurt?* However, this would come back to haunt me. Today was day 12.

I had my first massage today at the Macmillan Centre. As part of the support available, I was entitled to four free treatment sessions, and I had chosen to have massages. They were extremely relaxing; nothing like what I was used to from a sports massage, but certainly beneficial. I hadn't been sure when or if I would be allowed to have a sports massage, but since I could book this meant there was no obvious reason why I shouldn't have one.

I had another booking at the Macmillan Centre. It was called 'Look Good, Feel Better', and it was something I had been told about at my 'Demystifying Chemotherapy' session. Apparently, it was often fully booked, so I signed up early and timed the date to fit in with when I thought I would be well enough to attend.

There were 12 of us at the session. The first thing I noticed was that most of us still had our hair. Perhaps everyone had booked in early. I noticed that one woman was wearing a wig. It seemed obvious to me that it was a wig, and this made me wary about wearing one myself. Perhaps it would be less obvious to someone who wasn't looking for one. I sat next to a woman who had undergone four chemotherapy treatments. She had used the cold cap and had kept her hair, yet she said it was a lot thinner, was still falling out, was nowhere near the condition it used to be in and was a great deal greyer. This made me even more certain that it was the right decision for me not to wear a cold cap. She also had a PICC line in, and again, this provided more reassurance that I had made the correct decision, as she explained how she would come into the hospital for additional appointments to have it cleaned.

I'm not usually one for pampering parties, but we were given a large bag of skincare products and cosmetics, which had been kindly donated by various makeup manufacturers. After being shown how best to use them, we got to take them home.

Thursday 29th March
I continued with my daily 5- or 6-mile early morning runs local to my house. In the evening, I also managed a weights class. This was the first time I had been to one since my surgery, and the instructor commented on my new hairstyle. I explained why I had been away. The mobility had returned to my left shoulder, and I felt sufficiently confident to fully lift the weights above my head. I had a good session and promised myself that I would try to keep going. I cleaned all the weights with anti-bacterial wipes before use and regularly slathered on hand gel. I also chose a spot at the end of the room away from other people and close to the windows. My consultant had encouraged me to exercise. I would do my best to continue, but I needed to be vigilant about limiting my chance of catching anything. I would always stand away from crowds and was careful not to put my fingers near my mouth after touching anything. I also excessively washed my hands.

Day 15 came and went with no issues, but I noticed a little tenderness in my head, or was I just imagining it? I would twiddle my hair and pull it occasionally to see if it was going to come out, but it stayed put. Maybe it wasn't going to happen. After all, my symptoms so far weren't too bad compared with what I had read and heard about from others. Maybe it would be the same for my hair loss.

Ellen, the ultra-running friend who had visited me just after my surgery, had posted on social media a picture of her hair shaved all over to a grade 4. She was preparing for her 615-mile run along Monarch's Way and didn't want to worry about looking after her hair. She looked amazing, but I didn't expect to look so good. I felt even more nervous about the prospect of losing my hair. Aware that having my hair falling out in clumps over several days could be traumatic, I decided I needed to take control of the situation. I messaged Ellen. Her wife, Lisa, always cut her hair for her and I asked if she would be able to do mine. I wanted to have it done in a friendly, supportive environment. They were away over the Easter bank holiday weekend, but Lisa agreed to cut it whenever I wanted after their return. I was happy because I now had a plan.

Friday 30th March
Day 16 post chemotherapy. Today was Good Friday, and my head felt a little sore. I noticed a few strands in the sink after cleaning my teeth, but it wasn't enough to worry about. I figured it would probably be OK until Ellen and Lisa got back from their trip.

Saturday 31st March
Day 17 post chemotherapy. I decided to do the very hilly Parkrun at Queen Elizabeth Country Park for the first time. Having regularly trained in the park, I knew it would be a tough one. It was also very muddy, and I managed to fall over along the route. After the run, I took off my buff and noticed it had some hair in it. I pulled a few strands at the back of my head, and they all came out in a little clump. My hair was currently about four inches long. I pulled at a few more strands and the same thing happened. It looked like it was going to

need cutting sooner than I had expected. After the run, I chatted with Russ and Angie over coffee and explained how hair was coming out at the back of my head but not at the front. When I tugged at some strands at the front to demonstrate, these came out too. They both laughed at me, and I shared in their mirth. I definitely needed to get a haircut!

Despite the fact I had been laughing, as we drove home from the park, the hair loss suddenly became a really big issue for me, and I began to cry. I didn't feel I could wait until after the bank holiday to have it cut, as I felt the trauma of my hair gradually coming out would be worse than chopping it off altogether (although strangely, I did quite enjoy pulling bits of my hair out). I hadn't cried much at all so far, but suddenly, I felt panicked and overwhelmed by what was about to happen. Perhaps I had been in denial or just too busy concentrating on other aspects of my treatment. I felt certain that I wanted to get my hair cut, but at the same time, I really didn't want to do it. It was a big step, and one there would be no turning back from. It felt far more significant than dying my hair from blonde to brown and getting it cut short, and it was very scary. Keen not to put it off, as soon as we got home, I went out and bought an electric razor before the shops closed.

Henry was staying with us that night, so Russ and I waited until he was in bed before getting the razor out. I sat with my head down, watching my hair fall to the floor as Russ shaved it to a number 5. I didn't really want to have it cut, but I knew I had to, and I just wanted to get it over with. When he had finished, Russ said it looked better than he had expected, but I wasn't yet ready to look.

It took me a while to pluck up the courage to face my reflection in the mirror. I went up to our bedroom to absorb my new look in my own good time. I suppose it was OK, but I didn't really like my new appearance. I felt it defined me somehow, and it made me appear ill.

I started trying my scarves on, but I wasn't happy with how any of them looked. Instead, I found one of my regular running buffs and refolded it so that it became more like a hat. This is a lot how I look when I'm out running anyway, so I felt more like my old self. I came back downstairs with the buff on my head and wore it for the rest of the evening while watching a film and acting like nothing had changed. I could pretend in my mind that nothing had happened to my hair and go on as normal with my head in the sand (or buff!) for a little while longer.

Sunday 1st April
In the morning, Henry came into our room after sleeping in the spare bedroom. He sat on the bed and said, 'Your hair is cut, Nanny.'

'Yes,' I replied. 'I needed to get it cut because it's falling out.'

As always, children accept things very quickly and are great levellers. Henry just carried on as normal, and while he was eating his breakfast in the lounge, he said, completely unprompted, 'I like your hair, Nanny.'

'Thank you, Henry,' I replied. 'It's OK, isn't it?'

If my three-year-old grandson thought it was OK then it must be OK, I decided, and somehow everything felt much easier after that.

Later that morning, Russ and I went for a run around Portsmouth. It was three days until my second chemotherapy session, and I was feeling back to my old self and able to run as normal. I was chuffed to manage 19 miles, which was even further than the half marathon I had done the previous weekend. I wore my buff as a band round my head and didn't worry about it. I looked much the same as I usually did, and I was happy enough knowing that no one would take any notice.

Chapter 4
Cycle 2

Wednesday 4th April

It had been three weeks since my last treatment, and having recovered from all the side effects, I was ready for my second dose of poison.

The process was quicker this time. I chatted to my friend Clare, who had come along to support me, whilst the nurse manually injected me with the bright red epirubicin. As my veins weren't as visible as they had been previously, a different vein in the side of my arm had to be used. My hands were cold, and a warm compress was used on my arm to make the veins dilate and, therefore, easier to see.

My blood levels were added to my personal chemotherapy booklet, and I looked through them carefully. My iron levels had dropped very slightly, but apart from that, every other indicator looked OK.

Over the following days, I wasn't so obsessive about using the special mouthwash. During the first cycle, I had used it from day one, and this time I decided to wait until three days in, and this seemed to help. I also found I did not need the salty mouth rinse, and during the first week, I found it easier to eat than I had done previously.

Again, sleep eluded me for a few days as the steroids worked their magic. They had been prescribed to help reduce the early side effects of the chemotherapy, but they came with their own adverse reactions, including lack of sleep, irritability, water retention and constipation, to name a few. However, the symptoms were now familiar to me and were consequently less of an issue.

Chapter 4 – Cycle 2

Saturday 7th April

Emma, my ultra running friend, was doing her final long run in preparation for her 100-mile race along the Thames Path in May. These comprised five-mile loops round Staunton Country Park, a lovely spot in Havant with plenty of wide trails through woods and fields and not as many hills as there are in our usual training place, Queen Elizabeth Country Park. As I was feeling well, I decided to join her for some of the loops.

Emma picked me up in the morning ready for an early start. She began her six-hour run while I went off to do the local Parkrun nearby. This was muddy in places, with a few inclines. I started steady to ensure that I saved some energy for running with Emma later, but as is often the case with Parkrun, the general awareness of it being a timed event pushed me on to run a little harder, and I told myself it would be good for my lungs. I needed to get my heart rate up rather than just plod along, so I had a good run and put a bit of effort in. I took off my buff at the end to cool off. I had a few bald patches now, and it was obvious that my short hair cut was not just by design. I noticed a few sideways glances in my direction, where people were trying to look without being obvious about it. Feeling self-conscious and uncomfortable, I promptly put my buff back on.

I was aware of my hair beginning to thin in places at the side of my head, and I was also experiencing some tenderness. I'd been told I could take some paracetamol, if necessary, but I didn't think it was that bad. If I went out running, I wore the buff over my entire head rather than using it as a headband. At other times, Russ would help tie my triangular head scarves on during the day, and I even had special ones for the evenings. I had purchased quite a few, as I wanted a choice of styles and to look relatively normal for every type of occasion. When I was running with a buff on my head, I looked no different to how I normally looked.

I joined Emma for her third five-mile loop, popped back home for some food and then returned to join her for her final one. Considering how far she had already run, she was still going strong. By the end, I had run a total of 12.5 miles, and I felt perfectly OK. Again, the steroids were probably helping to keep me feeling energised despite the lack of sleep. I didn't expect to feel so good the following day, and I had planned my running accordingly.

Sunday 8th April
Another steroid-induced early rise! Feeling tired now from the lack of sleep, the prospect of a run wasn't particularly appetising. I'd also started my five-day course of injections, which were designed to help with my neutrophil production. I managed an hour's run, an out and back one at Wickham, along a straight path that was once a railway line. Initially, it felt a bit of a trudge, and I ran with my head down and my music on to take my mind off the negativity I was feeling. However, once I had turned to go back, I began to feel better.

Coming into the second week of my cycle, I now knew what to expect, so I did my best to get out for a run without putting too much pressure on myself. I would pick out my running clothes the day before and make sure they were in view, which would force me to put them on, even if I didn't really feel like going out. If I hadn't slept well, I would go back to bed, rest a while longer and then try going for a run a little later.

Friday 13th April
On Tuesday, I had a telephone appointment with my doctor. He agreed that if the working-from-home arrangement was helpful then I should continue with it. She signed me off for up to a week after my final chemotherapy treatment, which removed my worry over work. I could work from home when I felt well enough and go into the office

if I needed to at weekends, when no one else was in, or at the end of a cycle when I was at my best.

Each run this week was a challenge, but I still managed to complete them without needing to walk.

Apart from running every morning, the rest of my days this week were spent resting. I found it difficult to concentrate on anything for long and, looking back, I don't really know where the time went each day.

Saturday 14th April
I drove to Lee-on-the-Solent to meet my friend Maria, who was doing her 50th Parkrun. It gave me the chance to catch up with her and her husband, whom I hadn't seen for ages. We'd worked together many years ago and remained long-term friends.

At the same point in my first cycle, I had managed to do a reasonable Parkrun at Southsea on the Saturday, followed by a half marathon the following day. I saw no reason why I couldn't have a good go at this Parkrun to see what I could manage. I did a short warm up, and although my legs felt quite heavy, I was determined to give it a go. I set off near the front to get away from the crowds. I no longer felt comfortable in large groups of people. In my mind, I was in a germ-ridden environment, and everyone had the potential of passing on some nasty cold or disease. I positioned myself to the side of the main mass of runners with my arms crossed, tightly hugging myself to minimise the chances of anyone touching me.

I found myself running quite strong, and I pushed to keep my pace fairly constant, catching up with and passing a few familiar runners in the second half. I knew I had run strong and was delighted to finish in a time that was only a few seconds off my best. Although I knew I would have my bad days, the chemotherapy so far wasn't completely stripping me of my strength.

Sunday 15th April
In the morning, I ran a steady 10 miles, and in the afternoon, I felt well enough to spend a few hours at work.

From this point on, I knew I would begin to improve a little each day. I felt well enough to do some reasonable runs and had recovered enough mentally to cope with working from home.

Thursday 19th April
I managed a nine-mile run around Queen Elizabeth Country Park. For a while, I was able to forget what was happening to me and enjoy the freedom of being on the trails. I was near the end of my second cycle and felt 'normal' again. I was able to spend more time cleaning in preparation for the next cycle. My obsession with not wanting to catch anything meant I wanted the house to be as clean and as bug free as possible. I knew that once I'd had my next treatment, I wouldn't feel like doing any housework. My next chemotherapy session was beginning to loom large. Although I knew I could cope with it, and I knew what to expect, the thought of it still filled me with dread. I hated injecting myself from day four to day eight, and it was always a great relief when that part of the treatment was over.

While absentmindedly scrolling through Facebook, I came across a post from one of my old rowing buddies, Sarah. The last time we'd messaged each other was three years earlier, and I hadn't seen her for 27 years. We'd both rowed at Thames Tradesmen Rowing Club, which is based near Barnes Bridge alongside the river Thames. We had trained together and raced in various events, including at Henley Women's Regatta and internationally at Ghent, as well as at several, more local UK regattas. Sarah continued to live by the Thames and had gone much further with her rowing than me. I left the rowing scene when I went to study physics at Nottingham University.

Chapter 4 – Cycle 2

Although I did some running and completed my first half marathon, my exercise became quite sporadic as I focused on my studies.

Sarah's long Facebook post stopped me in my tracks. She was letting everyone know that she was just about to embark on her final chemotherapy session for breast cancer. She thanked everyone who had been there for her during the diagnosis, surgery and chemotherapy, and she was now letting her wider circle of friends know about her condition, which she'd generally kept quiet about. Following chemotherapy, she was going to start radiotherapy, and she reminded everyone to get themselves checked. She'd had a routine mammogram at 50, and that was how her cancer had been detected.

I planned to message her and let her know that I was in the same situation. However, before I got round to it, my brother, who also knew Sarah, messaged her with my news, and she immediately reached out to me. She'd had a very similar diagnosis, but she'd had to have separate surgeries for the tumour and the lymph nodes, and she'd also had a portacath inserted, which extended the time between diagnosis and chemotherapy. A portacath is a device that is placed beneath the skin. It's fitted in the right side of the chest under anaesthetic and is attached to a catheter that is threaded into a large vein above the right side of the heart. A needle can then be inserted into the port to draw blood or give fluids. This is an alternative to a PICC line, and it can be left in place for months, and possibly even years if required. Sarah had been diagnosed in August 2017, and she had been off work since the following October. She was not due back until July 2018. Her chemotherapy drugs were the same as mine, and she was due to start radiotherapy at the end of May. We exchanged many text messages discussing and comparing the various aspects of our treatment and experiences, and then later agreed to meet up before my fourth chemotherapy cycle and before she started her radiotherapy.

So far, I had not connected with anyone who had been through, or was going through, the same as me. I hadn't felt the need to, and I also figured that even if they were experiencing the exact same thing, they wouldn't understand the amount of exercise I was doing. However, I knew Sarah would understand. After all, we had known each other when we were both in our 20s and at the peak of fitness. Now I felt like I had someone that I could go to for advice. Sarah had coped well throughout her chemotherapy. She only had one issue with her first docetaxel cycle (cycle number four). She ultimately believed her starting level of fitness and positive attitude had had a lot to do with this. From that point on, we kept in touch throughout our treatment journeys.

Saturday 21st April
It was the final weekend before my third treatment. Russ had a 22-mile run planned, so I decided to join him. We parked our car at the Hayling ferry near Southsea and ran the 15 miles all the way round to Hayling to catch the ferry back to our car. Russ was running at a steady 10-minutes-per-mile pace, which included two-minute walk breaks every 13 minutes. It's a running style that I am familiar with, having used this approach for some of my own ultra events. Russ's steady pace made it easy for me to cope, and as we progressed, I felt more confident that I could continue for his entire run. I found myself smiling inwardly at the fact I was still able to do this. After getting off the ferry, Russ and I continued to run another seven miles along the Southsea seafront. It was a gorgeous sunny day. We bumped into friends along the beach and happily chatted with them. I felt tired from the run but was perfectly fine otherwise, if a little euphoric.

The next day, I accompanied Russ on his run once again. This time, it was over 15 miles, and again I found that I felt comfortable throughout. I was over the moon. I had managed to run a 60-mile week. This was beyond my wildest expectations. I was coping far better than I (and no doubt anyone else) could have expected.

At this point, I decided to increase my iron tablets to two a day. I'd had another period during this cycle, and then after a week's break found that I was having yet another one, which ended up continuing for nearly two weeks. It wasn't as heavy as before but was yet another side effect of the chemotherapy... a gift that just keeps on giving.

Tuesday 24th April
It was the day before my third chemotherapy treatment. I ventured out for a morning run with the knowledge that now was when I'd be feeling the best I possibly could. I ran strong and with a sense of purpose. It was both exhilarating and invigorating, and I managed to keep the dread of what was to come out of my mind for a short while. I had put sunblock on, as I had been told that it was important to protect myself from the sun due to heightened sensitivity whilst on chemotherapy.

The hair on the side of my head had disappeared completely, and all that was left was a small, dark patch of hair at the centre of the top of my head. Although I had grown accustomed to it, I was aware it looked odd, and so I chose to wear a hat of some description whenever I was outside. Russ cut my hair down to a number two to make the patch look less strange. It would be a while now before I'd have a full head of hair again. It would be interesting to see how it grew back. Would it be all grey? Would it initially be curly? I had been told that following chemotherapy, it's quite common for hair to grow back differently. Only time would tell.

Chapter 5
Cycle 3 / Thames Path 100

Wednesday 25th April

As I had done with the last two cycles, I went for a run on the morning of my chemotherapy treatment. I was aware of how 'normal' I was feeling and knew how I would soon be feeling a lot worse, but I had managed OK so far, so I tried to push this thought to the back of my mind.

Emma, my ultra-running friend who I had recently run with around Staunton Country Park, met me at home and walked with me down to my third session – my last FEC cycle. It was a slightly longer wait than the last time, but this gave us a good opportunity to chat. We discussed her Thames Path 100 challenge, and we were both excited by the prospect. Emma was working towards finishing the 100-mile race in under 24 hours.

I had previously agreed to buddy Emma for the last 20 or so miles of the race, but in the aftermath of my diagnosis, I pulled out. However, I was now more confident that I would be able to run through my treatment and we agreed that I would buddy her for the last 10 miles, from Abingdon to the finish at Oxford.

She was just about to have her last low mileage weekend, 10 miles on both Saturday and Sunday, at a comfortable, relaxing pace. She agreed to come and join me for a run on Saturday.

The days post chemotherapy were similar to how they'd been previously, and this familiarity made them easier to deal with. It was beginning to feel more like following a routine, and this provided some comfort. I continued with the anti-sickness tablets twice a day

Chapter 5 – Cycle3 / Thames Path 100

for the first three days, but again did not experience any significant feelings of nausea. I just had the usual waking up in the early hours because of the four days' worth of steroids. This time, I was given an extra supply of steroids to take away with me and take during the next cycle. This would be my first dose of docetaxel, and I was told I needed to start taking the steroids the day before treatment rather than on the day itself. I noticed that I was given only three days' supply so I surmised (wrongly) that the side effects would be fewer.

Friday 27th April

As usual, we had Henry with us for most of the day. Whilst out shopping with him, we stopped for a coffee. I was feeling a little hot (I found that, generally, my temperature would rise a little a day or two after my chemotherapy), and I took my hat off to cool down. As usual, Henry wasn't particularly bothered. I had explained that my hair was coming out because of the medicine I was taking and that it would grow back. He asked if he could feel my head, so once I had wiped his sticky hands with an antibacterial wipe he came over and gently rubbed the top of my scalp, completely unfazed by the whole experience. Sitting with Russ, it didn't bother me to have my hat off, but I suspected others were staring. Russ told me there was someone looking who also had a hat on, and he was sure they were also on treatment. I wondered if my doing this had been of any help to them, as they could see that it was OK not to wear a hat and that children were fine with it, as they seem to adapt the easiest to change. When I had told my 24-year-old son about my diagnosis, he was generally fine about it too. He had said, 'If you're not worried about it, Mum, then I'm not', which seemed like a very pragmatic approach to take.

Saturday 28th April

Exactly three weeks to the day, I went back to Staunton Country Park to run some more loops. Last time, I'd done the Parkrun before supporting Emma for a couple of her loops. This time, I was planning to do three five-mile loops with Russ. It was a little more mileage but at a slightly slower pace, and it did not include the Parkrun. Based on my current energy levels, I surmised that I was up to doing it.

Russ was doing a six-hour run. He would do an hour on his own then Emma and I would join him for two loops. Rob, one of his planned buddy runners for the GUCR, was coming along for loops three to five, and then I would join him again for his final loop. This worked really well. Emma got her easy, stress free, pre-Thames Path run at a conversational pace, and Russ had company for all but the first of his loops.

Sunday 29th April
The steroids continued to stop me sleeping. I forced myself to stay in bed until 4am to make sure that I had some rest.

Later that morning, Russ and I went to Queen Elizabeth Country Park and did a two-hour run along the trails and back. I found it quite challenging. I could tell my energy levels were dropping.

We had arranged for my dad to stay at his brother's in Morecambe for a couple of weeks, which would give me a break from visiting him for a while. Two weeks ago, we had dropped him off at Watford, where other members of the family had picked him up to drive him North. We now had to go back to Watford to bring him home again. I agreed to do some of the driving, and despite the lack of sleep, I was still wide awake. The steroids were doing their stuff! By the time we finished the four-hour round trip, I was exhausted and desperate to get some sleep. However, it eluded me again, and I found myself crying with exhaustion and frustration. I desperately wanted some proper rest, but my body just wouldn't let me have it.

Chapter 5 – Cycle3 / Thames Path 100

Monday 30th April

As a regular runner, I am used to coming home from work in the evening and forcing myself out for a run, despite feeling tired. One saying that has always stayed in my head is, 'You never regret going for a run.' I had enough experience to know that I would always feel glad having completed a run and would regret it if I didn't. I had made the decision that my treatment was not going to beat me. My aim was never to miss a planned run. I would struggle to get started, but inevitably, the exercise would help to pull me out from any fatigue I was feeling.

Wednesday 2nd May

The midweek weather forecast wasn't great. Temperatures were reasonable but there was persistent rain. I could leave my run until later, but that would change the routine I had grown accustomed to during the early stages of my chemotherapy cycle. I drove to Farlington Marshes, a nature reserve a couple of miles from home. I put my raincoat on, stuck my hood up and put in my earphones to get me through the trudge ahead. It was hard to get myself going, but with music in my ears and my head down and hidden in my raincoat, I plodded slowly along my familiar route, struggling against the drugs inside me and fighting the lethargy and the uncomfortable sensations in my mouth. Initially, it was difficult to do anything more than plod along lost in my own negativity, but after a mile or so, I took my hood off and let the rain hit my face. It felt refreshing, and instead of being shut up in my own small world, it was good to look around me at the landscape and the sea. I began to relax. This is what running always does for me when I'm feeling low. Having stopped looking down at the floor, I now felt stronger and more positive. As I turned and ran back, I felt much more like my usual self. I was now running as I normally would, with a steady pace rather than a lazy plod. I was feeling energised and ready to face the rest of the day. During my treatment, this was how it always seemed to be on the most difficult mornings.

Saturday 5th May
It was the day of Emma's 100-mile run along the Thames Path. The weather forecast predicted a gorgeous morning and afternoon ahead, but for an ultra run, this isn't really a good thing.

Russ and I arrived early at Richmond Town Hall, so that Russ could help out with the kit check, which involved ensuring that the participants had their mandatory equipment with them, including a head torch and an emergency blanket. I said hi to a few people and then went back outside to keep away from the crowds of runners that were shortly due to arrive. It was the tenth day since my last chemotherapy treatment, and the time when I was most vulnerable, when my body would not be able to fight off infection. I rejected any offers of a hug from people I had not seen in a while. I felt uncomfortable doing this, but I didn't want to risk getting ill. I had done well so far, and I wanted to keep it that way. I had a buff on, which completely covered my head, so to anyone who didn't know me, I looked fairly normal and blended in with the increasing crowds. Someone asked if I could take a picture for them, and I instinctively agreed to take their phone to do it. Saying no would appear rude, and they wouldn't understand. Subsequently, I decided to sit a bit further out of the way so that nobody would trouble me again.

I had put on my bright orange sweat top from the Thames Ring 250. I didn't usually wear it, but I had recently been reminded that I should show it off with pride rather than allowing it to languish in the cupboard. As a result, while I was sitting out of the way, minding my own business, someone came up to me. He recognised the top. He had finished Thames Ring in the same year. We had met on the route

Chapter 5 – Cycle3 / Thames Path 100

when I borrowed his phone to make a call after losing my mobile. We'd had a bacon sandwich together at Banbury Station. He asked me how I was doing. I proceeded to tell him that I had breast cancer, and I lifted up a bit of my buff to show him my bald head. I saw the familiar look of shock on his face, as if I had just told him I'd been handed a death sentence, and I immediately attempted to reassure him that everything was fine. We chatted a little longer, but I decided telling him had been the wrong decision, as it had made him feel awkward. I vowed to stop mentioning it to acquaintances. I hated the 'look' I got.

Emma had stayed overnight at a nearby hotel, and I walked over to meet her and help her carry her bags. She was excited about the run and was very chatty and energetic, as always. She had worked hard for this. I was looking forward to meeting her at Abingdon the following morning, 90 miles into her 100-mile run. I had no doubt she would get there, but I was worried about my own part. I had the responsibility of getting her through her last 10 miles. I had to make sure that we didn't get lost and that I got the best out of her. How I would do this was something I would decide at the time, once I saw how she was coping. There are no hard and fast rules when it comes to buddying a runner on an ultra.

For today, though, I had agreed to 'sweep' eight miles of the route. The purpose of a sweeper is to follow the route behind the last runner and clear all the markers set out to help people follow the course. Russ was sweeping for 22 miles from the start at Richmond to Wraysbury. I would then take over and sweep for the next eight miles to Dorney Lake.

The runners all set off at 10am, with Russ following 15 minutes later. It would take him about six hours to sweep his part of the course, so I went off to find a pub near Shepperton Lock, where I could sit outside, have a drink and watch the runners passing by. It was a beautiful sunny day. Spring had finally sprung, and it had come with a vengeance. It was going to be the hottest Early May Bank Holiday we had seen since records began. So hot, in fact, that this race would see the highest dropout rate at a centurion event. But I knew Emma would be fine. She was made of tough stuff, and I knew I would be seeing her at Abingdon the next morning. At exactly what time was currently unknown, but we were working on a 7am arrival to give her the best chance of completing the race in under 24 hours.

I drove on to Wraysbury to meet Russ. I tried unsuccessfully to have a sleep in the car but managed to at least relax for half an hour before getting changed and walking to the checkpoint. Russ wasn't due for another hour, so I decided to walk backwards along the course to meet him. It was very hot for running but a perfect day for a stroll along the Thames. I had put on a white peaked cap and loads of sunblock to protect me from the sun. I met Russ at Staines and then turned to go back with him behind the last runner.

At Wraysbury, I saw my friend, Leanne. I had not seen her for a long time. Despite being in third place, she had decided to pull out of the race. We chatted for a while, but this time, I decided to keep quiet about my breast cancer diagnosis. However, she noted my short hair under my hat and asked about my new hairstyle. I then had to explain and be in receipt of that shocked look. But this look was slightly different. It was also a look of guilt for what she considered must have been a thoughtless comment, and I had to tell her that it was fine in addition to reassuring her about my diagnosis. It seemed that not saying anything was no better than being upfront about it. There was no best or easy way to deal with my diagnosis when meeting people. I would just have to take each situation as it came and deal with any awkwardness that arose.

Chapter 5 – Cycle3 / Thames Path 100

Russ and I parted at Wraysbury, and I continued alone with a plastic bag and some scissors to remove the course markers as I went. The last runner was just ahead of me and was walking very slowly. I could tell by his gait that he had had enough. His walking pace would mean that he wouldn't make the cut off at the next checkpoint. I chatted with him and asked what was wrong. He was a little wobbly on his feet and said that the heat was getting to him. I got him to retrieve his buff from his backpack, soak it with water and put it over the back of his neck. To try and take his mind off his woes, I asked him why he was doing this event. He had entered it a while ago but later cancelled. Having discovered the cancellation was unsuccessful, he decided he might as well just do it. He was heavily set and told me how much weight he had already lost and how many marathons he had completed. Having already done a 100k race, this was the next step. However, since he had entered, his wife had left him, and his training had taken a nosedive. The chatting made him forget about how rough he was feeling for a while, and I noticed his walking improve. The encounter reminded me how everyone has their story to tell in these races, whether they are at the front or the back of the pack. I told him about my own situation and said I would be looking for his number at the finish. However, a few miles before the check point at Dorney, he rang a friend, who had been supporting him, and asked him to come and pick him up.

Having walked for some miles now, I ran on, collecting markers and trying to catch up with the next back marker. Russ met me at Dorney Lake, and we drove to our B&B near Abingdon.

Emma's progress through the day went exactly to plan. I had booked our room to ensure I got my rest, but now I couldn't sleep. I worried about not meeting her in time, about getting her lost and letting her down. At least Russ was managing to sleep.

Sunday 6th May
I got a call at 5am from Emma's crew saying she was expected to be at Abingdon at 6:30am, ahead of schedule and poised to finish in under 24 hours. The question now was: how far under 24 hours she could get?

She arrived at Abingdon before 6:20am, so a sub-23-hour finish was on the cards. She just needed to keep on doing what she was doing. I was fully aware that despite having only 10 miles to go, for Emma it would seem like an eternity. She had been pushing her limits for over 20 hours, and I would be asking her for even more. She knew that would be my aim, and with only two to three miles to go, she did have a couple of wobbles. She was exhausted and knew that she would be pushed, and even though that's what she wanted, her unconscious mind would come out with things to make me feel sorry for her and let her walk for a while. But I'd played these tricks myself with my buddies, so after a few more moans about how much further it was, I firmly told her to stop looking at her watch and just deal with it. I don't think it was what she expected to hear from me, and from there on in she managed to push through to an amazing time of 22 hours and 25 minutes. She came sixth in the overall female category. A fantastic achievement.

I chatted briefly with a few friends and then Russ drove us both home. I had my buff over my head, and for this weekend, to outsiders, I was just another buddy runner doing my bit for a friend. It was a perfect weekend.

I rested the following day and then continued with my daily running. The weather was sensational and for a short while, all my runs felt comfortable.

Chapter 5 – Cycle3 / Thames Path 100

Thursday 10th May

The day had finally arrived for my friend Sarah to visit me in Portsmouth. It would be the first time we'd seen each other for 27 years. She was currently three months ahead of me in her breast cancer journey, and we chatted about our diagnoses. Some aspects were similar, and others differed. Sarah was 52 and a fit lady, but her nurse had told her not to exercise. She was annoyed about this, as she had lost her fitness and put on weight (she went for a five-mile run as soon as she returned home after seeing me). Her surgery had been a little more complex, and she had needed two operations. She had been asked whether she would like reconstruction surgery on her 'normal' breast so that it was uplifted to match the other one. I had not been asked about this, but it was not something I really wanted anyway. She was also given sleeping tablets to combat the side-effects of the steroids. I would now have to ask about that too! She had worn a cold cap and still had a good crop of hair (although she said she had lost half of it), and she had dyed it with Holland and Barrett natural dye – something I had never even considered. She was happy to sit out in the sun whereas I had been told to avoid it. There were clearly differences in the advice we had been given. We compared our chemotherapy booklets, which showed the drugs we had been prescribed. The quantity of her chemotherapy drugs at each treatment was more than mine, but that was because she was heavier than me. I noticed how much docetaxel she had been given, and she told me how she'd had a very bad reaction to the first cycle and had ended up in A&E with suspected neutropenic sepsis. Following this, her dose was reduced by 25% and she had no further issues. We had a fantastic catch up, which included looking through some old photos and reminiscing. We promised we would not leave it another 27 years until the next time we met! It was good to talk to another cancer patient – one who was also an old friend – and compare experiences. Perhaps I should have considered this earlier. There were cancer groups available through Macmillan and various Facebook forums I could have tried, but generally, I had found my own way of coping.

Sunday 13th May
My weekend runs with Russ were 22 and 12 miles, respectively. Based on my chemotherapy cycle, this weekend was to be my big mileage weekend and would bring my weekly total to 59 miles. On the morning of my Sunday run, I woke up early, as I often did. My mind was churning with worry, and I'd broken out into a sweat. As the time for our run drew nearer, I was aware that my head felt hot. I took my temperature for the second time since starting the chemotherapy. It was 37.5C. What temperature did you have to reach before calling the Oncology Hotline for neutropenic sepsis? Oh, yes, above 38C. I wasn't there yet. I looked up the other symptoms related to the condition – feeling fluey, signs of infection, persistent diarrhoea or vomiting, shortness of breath, a sore mouth and bleeding or bruising. I had none of these. Perhaps these were simply menopausal hot flushes brought on by the chemotherapy. I decided I would ask the nurse the following day and deal with it for now so that Russ wouldn't worry too much. Though he was already worried, he knew better than to suggest I should stay at home and rest. We ran for an hour out and back along the Wickham disused railway trail. We both took music and ran in our own head space. It suited me. I had taken a couple of paracetamols to see if that would help bring my temperature down. It wasn't easy, and I found it hard to fully relax. I felt more under the weather than I typically did at this point post chemo, but I had run 22 miles the previous day so what could I expect?

As I was in my 'good week', I came home and rested for an hour before going into work while the office was empty. But I still wasn't feeling that good. I got stuck into reading my emails and other work

Chapter 5 – Cycle3 / Thames Path 100

and found that the symptoms started to fade. By the time I left, three hours later, I felt much more like my old self.

Monday 14th May
I had my blood test followed by my pre-chemotherapy appointment. This time, I was armed with a mountain of questions for the breast care nurse, about sleeping tablets, haemorrhoids, anaemia, hot flushes and radiotherapy. She answered my queries and put me at ease. She also explained how there were new breath hold techniques that would reduce the risk to the heart during radiotherapy. Only my radiotherapy consultant could inform me of the risks specific to me. The nurse explained how it was likely I would need some radiotherapy on the lymph nodes in my neck. This was news to me! Yet more unexpected information I knew nothing about.

The breast care nurse filled me in about the next drug, docetaxel, which I would take over my following three cycles. At different times in the cycle, it would bring new symptoms, as well as some of the old, familiar ones. Early on post chemotherapy, I would have diarrhoea, so the issue I'd been having with piles would probably resolve itself. (Through each of the FEC cycles, a pattern had formed of being constipated while taking the steroids and then suffering with piles. A week or so in, I'd develop diarrhoea, when the piles would settle.) My joint aches and sore hands and feet would develop at around day five. The sore mouth would now affect me later, in about the second week. I would have to deal with a change in my routine, but at least I knew a little of what to expect. I had already started to paint my nails dark in preparation for this cycle. I had been told they would be sensitive to sunlight and would get damaged if I didn't do this. My weight was stable, as I compensated for the early weeks of eating less by eating out more often at the end of the cycle, when my infection risk was lower, and I felt more like myself. It was nearly time for my next emotional and physical battle. I walked out of the appointment and held back the tears. Yet again, the unknown was overwhelming. I parked the tears for now and walked home. I would take it one day at a time and get up and get out as planned. I would cope with this and deal with whatever came my way. I was taking more naps now, and again, I'd woken up early with a sweat on. It looked like my sleeping pattern was going to be affected even more. I was halfway there, though, and I had coped so far. I told myself I would continue to cope.

Tuesday 15th May
I woke up early feeling hot and uncomfortable. I took my first dose of steroids. There may only have been three days' worth this time, but now I had to take twice the dose. I was having hot flushes, but my temperature was OK. Following the hot flushes, I'd feel very cold again. Was it the menopausal symptoms or something more sinister? For the time being, I would settle on the former.

I took myself out for an early morning run. My legs felt heavy, and my breathing was more laboured. I could easily just be tired from my weekend of long-distance running, but currently there was no way to know. The views today were stunning. Running alongside rapeseed fields that would soon be gone, I savoured how wonderful it was to be out. Later in the year, when the nights drew in, I wouldn't be able to do this off-road run.

When I got home, I promptly had a bath and went back to bed for an hour, where I slept soundly. When I awoke, I was feeling groggy, and the thought of going to the gym did not enthuse me. I recognised this feeling as one that I would typically have in the first week of my chemotherapy cycle rather than the last. However, as always, I got up, got out and went. I told my trainer that I was feeling more tired than usual, and that I'd done a run that morning. He put me on an exercise

Chapter 5 – Cycle3 / Thames Path 100

bike and had me cycling for about 20 minutes with the resistance at a level where I could still talk comfortably. This pulled me from my fog and lethargy. After that I did some weights, repeating with each repetition, 'You're not going to beat me.'

I had always disliked the term 'battling cancer', as it meant someone has either beaten cancer or lost their battle. A tumour is discovered, and its location, type and size impact the prognosis, as does whether the cancer has spread. I didn't consider this a battle. You have the treatment, and you deal with the treatment, and either the cancer cells are destroyed, or they are not. I believed that you had no control over this, and whether you had a positive mental attitude or not would make no difference to the state of your original cancer and whether it would spread. However, after the last few days, I was beginning to see that I was engaged in a battle, and it was both a physical and a mental one. I fought every day against the lethargy that had me wanting to go back to bed in the morning, after being up since 4am. Every day I would get up and run knowing that today I had beaten it, and every day I made it to the gym, I reminded myself again how I had won. But equally, walking instead of running didn't mean that it had beaten me. Russ always reminds me that I am too hard on myself, not to mention extremely stubborn. Cancer is an ever-changing platform and involves constant knockbacks. There are so many cancer groups and counselling options to help people deal with their diagnosis, but I used my running as my strategy to take back some control over the situation. If I could run, then cancer hadn't won, and I remained in charge of my life on a day-to-day basis. Every morning I would dust myself down and get ready for the next battle. Every day I made a choice over how my day would be. The cup was half empty or the cup was half full. But throughout the journey, there were many changes that provided new challenges to deal with. I could tell that my emotions were a little closer to the edge now, and that it would be so easy to falter and let the cancer win just for one day. But for now, I wanted to win. Not just in the long term but every single day. Every day was mine to live how I chose. They could still be good days if I wanted them to be.

After going to the gym, I ate well and decided that I wouldn't work today. It was gorgeous outside, so I sat under an umbrella in the front garden and continued writing my diary. In addition to my running, this had also become my therapy and was helping me to get through the process one day and one step at a time.

1. One mile left to go of the 250-mile Thames Ring Ultra – June 2017

2. Our wedding day – 5th August 2017

3. First Female Over 50 at the Druid's 3-Day Ultra – 12th November 2017

4. Female over 50 winner at the Winter Cross 50k Ultra – 28th December 2017

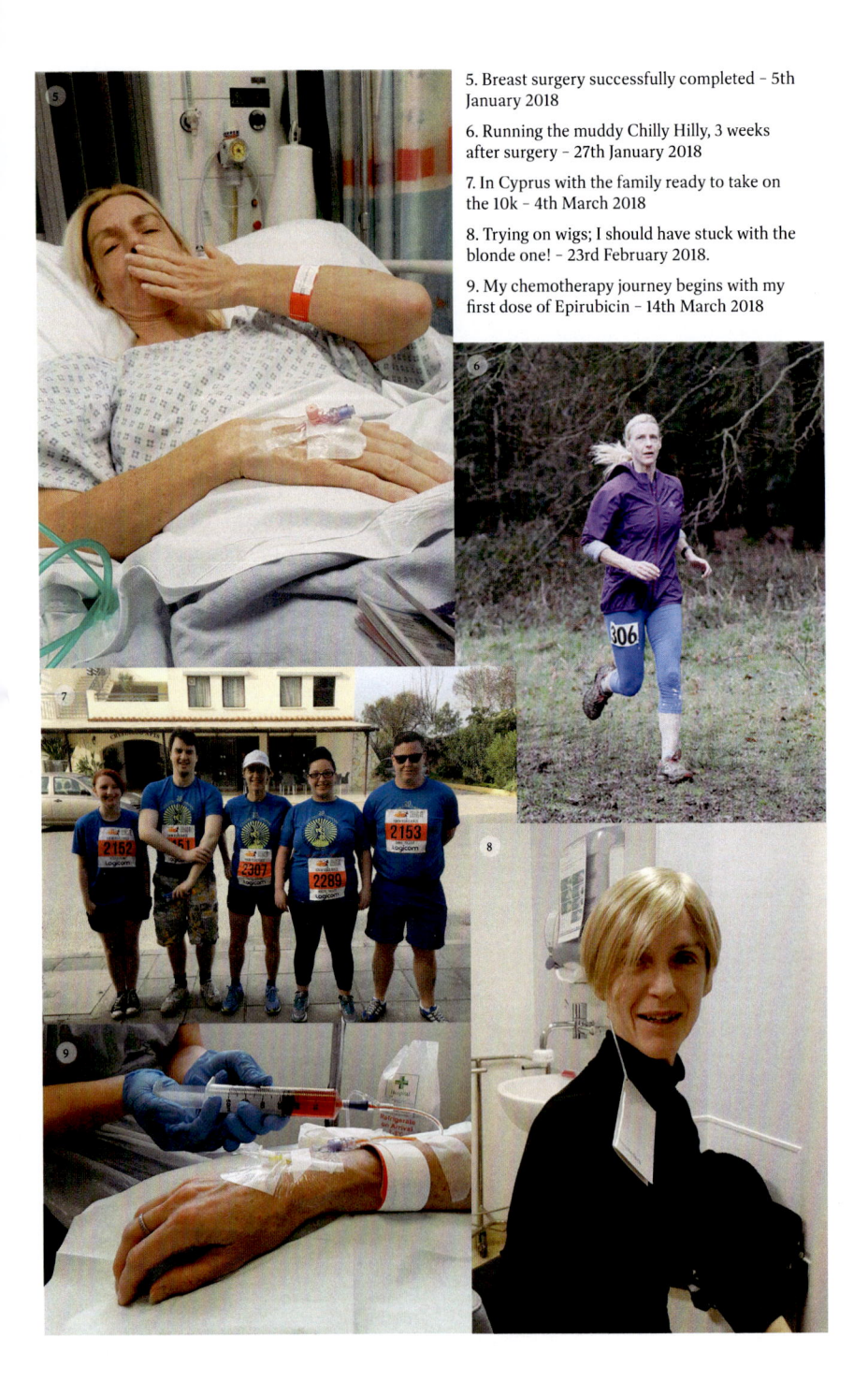

5. Breast surgery successfully completed – 5th January 2018

6. Running the muddy Chilly Hilly, 3 weeks after surgery – 27th January 2018

7. In Cyprus with the family ready to take on the 10k – 4th March 2018

8. Trying on wigs; I should have stuck with the blonde one! – 23rd February 2018.

9. My chemotherapy journey begins with my first dose of Epirubicin – 14th March 2018

10. Getting a crew cut as my hair starts to fall out – 30th March 2018

11. On the Hayling Ferry mid 22-mile run covering my partially bald head – 21st April 2018

12. At the end of Thames Path 100 with Emma Bird after buddying her for the last 10 miles – 6th May 2018

13. Catching up with Sarah Kell after many years and comparing our cancer journeys – 8th May 2018

14. In hospital for the second time with suspected neutropaenia – 24th May 2018

105

15. Running the Ladies 5 with my good friend Angie Agate - 10th June 2018
16. Proudly showing off our Ladies 5 medals - photo courtesy of David Brawn - 10th June 2018
17. Celebrating the wedding of our good friends, Mich and Amy, with my 'new hair growth' - 22nd September 2018

18. Russ on the start line of Spartathlon, his dream race – 28th September 2018
19. Second over 50 lady at the Cyprus Marathon, 7 months after radiotherapy – March 2019
20. At the finish of GUCR eating the 'Screw Cancer' chocolate trophy - May 2019

21. Waiting at the start of Spartathlon with my husband Russ and good friend Mich, with the Parthenon in the background - 30th Sept 2022

22. Finally running Spartathlon rather than watching from the sideline

23. Mile 58 of Spartathlon with the ruins from Ancient Corinth in the background

Chapter 6
Cycle 4

Wednesday 16th May

For my fourth cycle, Alex, my friend of over 40 years, came to stay and keep me company. It was great to catch up. We drove to Southsea seafront for breakfast in the 'Coffee Cup' overlooking the ocean and chatted easily. Where had all the years gone? Alex attended my first wedding in 1991 and my second 26 years later. We hatched a plan to visit a close mutual friend once my treatment had ended. She had only texted me once since my diagnosis and appeared to find it difficult to know what to say. I wanted to go and see her when I was well so I wouldn't make her feel uncomfortable. She is a really close friend, and I didn't mind the lack of contact. Everyone deals with cancer differently, and I understood that perhaps she found it difficult to know what to do or say. Russ helped out at a race recently and many people had asked after me. They were clearly concerned but felt they couldn't contact me due to their fears over how bad I might be. He would reassure them that I was doing really well, and this would put them at ease. Plenty of other people did stay in touch, so it was fine by me that some preferred not to.

    Whilst sitting with Alex, I received intermittent texts from people wishing me well for my fourth chemotherapy treatment. Some were straightforward, and I would answer back. A friend texted to warn me to take off my rings, as her mum, who'd had breast cancer, remembered that her fingers swelled up with the docetaxel. That made sense. The nurse had told me the extra steroids were partly to help with the swelling that would develop in my legs and ankles, but

I hadn't even considered that this would extend to my fingers.

Sometimes, I would get the 'How are you feeling?' texts, which I would find difficult to answer. I would leave them for a while and reply later, when I'd had time to think how best to respond. My feelings were complex and fluid, and I found it easier to answer with some facts about what was going on, and only when I was feeling positive. I saved my more negative concerns for a select few. I limited the number of people I let down my guard with, but equally, I was mostly positive about things. I thought about the people I hadn't yet told about my diagnosis. There were a couple of people who I rarely contacted but still considered good friends. I was just about ready to get round to letting them know. I understood why my friend, Sarah, who was just about to start her radiotherapy, had left sharing her news until she was nearly through her chemotherapy. Everyone must deal with their diagnosis and treatment in their own way. Yet here was Sarah still checking up on me by messenger and wishing me luck.

I had expected my chemotherapy appointment to be quick, as this time only one drug was to be administered via a pump. However, it ended up being the longest wait so far. The nurses, always busy, were even more rushed off their feet than usual, and I didn't get my cannula fitted until two hours after my actual appointment time. The docetaxel took an hour to be administered and was followed by a saline flush. After arriving for my appointment at 1.30pm, I didn't get home until gone six.

Despite their hectic schedule, the nurses, as always, were wonderful. They gave me an Imodium-like drug to deal with any possible diarrhoea, and the steroids to start taking ahead of the following cycle. They also gave me three sleeping tablets, which were to help me sleep whilst on the steroids.

'I wish I'd known about these before', I said to one of the nurses.

Chapter 6 – Cycle 4

'That's why we always ask you these questions, to know how you are coping,' she replied.

But no one had ever asked about my sleep. I just thought it was something I had to deal with.

The nurse gave me my blood levels from my appointment two days ago. My haemoglobin levels had reduced further – to 110. This explained why my running was a little more laboured, but it was something I could deal with. Typical haemoglobin levels for women are in the region of 120 to 150. I had been anaemic previously, with a haemoglobin level of 90, so I knew what it felt like. On the other hand, my white blood cell and neutrophil counts were good.

'The injections are working,' the nurse said.

This time, I was given a seven-day supply of injections, which would boost my neutrophils even further (or more likely I'd been given the additional supply because the new chemotherapy drug would have a more destructive effect on them). I looked at the quantity of docetaxel and noted that it was similar to the dose Sarah had been given. On her first docetaxel cycle, she developed neutropenic sepsis and ended up in A&E. Her dose was reduced by 25% for her subsequent two cycles. I questioned the dose with the nurse, and she said that everyone reacts differently. She also said that the exercise I was doing would help limit my side effects. She was very reassuring, so I decided to get on with keeping on top of my medication, continuing with my exercise and seeing what happened.

I was now completely bald. A surprising outcome from having no hair was how wonderful it felt to have the wind sweep over my head. The sensation of the breeze touching my hair follicles can only be described as sensual. It was a novel experience that I would not have felt had I chosen to wear the cold cap. Although distressing at times, I would look back at my period of hair loss and say that overall, it was a positive learning experience. I was now feeling excited over how my new hair would grow back.

Thursday 17th May
I had my first bout of diarrhoea. I had been warned about this, and it certainly came on quickly. I took my anti-sickness tablet before breakfast and my increased dose of steroids after it and set off on my 10-mile run. The last time I had covered this route was on a Sunday with Russ, when there had been a biting wind in the air, and it had felt more like 20 miles. This time, the weather was gorgeous, not too hot but a lovely sunny day. I found the first hill made me a little breathless, so I walked some of it. I ran with a smile on my face. The day was beautiful and I was doing what I loved. I knew how crucial running had become to my ability to cope with what I was going through. I was a little slower than usual, but I still felt upbeat and was grateful for the fact I was still able to run into my fourth cycle.

The steroids were keeping me upbeat, and I decided to go to my weights class without a hat on so that everyone would see my bald head. Today, I didn't care. I got loads of not-so-discreet looks whilst waiting for the class to start. I wanted people to see that a chemotherapy patient could still go to the gym and workout and be strong. Doing this made me feel empowered. I had nothing to be ashamed of. The instructor was the only one who already knew what I was going through, so she was not particularly surprised and had a little chat with me before the class started. I'm not sure I would have felt so confident on a different day without the steroids, but today I felt good.

Friday 18th May
My sleeping tablet knocked me out from nine until three, and I managed to stay in bed for an extra hour after that. I wasn't sure if I was getting more sleep than I'd managed while not taking the

Chapter 6 – Cycle 4

medication, but they did help send me into a deep sleep quickly. As it was a Friday, we had Henry with us, and Russ was trying to do some work at the back of our house. The steroids were keeping me awake and making me agitated. I tried to rest whilst everyone was busy around me but found this hard. I didn't want to go up to the bedroom, I just wanted some peace. Russ was trying to let me rest but seeing him busy made me feel guilty. Equally, I resented that my quiet space and usual routine was being disrupted, though this wasn't really his fault. The chemotherapy and the medication I was taking to combat the side effects were having an impact. However, I felt annoyed that Russ was trying to go about as normal. *What about me?* I thought. *You should be putting me first.* But perhaps I wasn't really being reasonable. I generally found Fridays harder than the rest of the week because I was taken out of my own routine and no longer had the house to myself, but I had never complained before. An occasional nap kept me going. I realised how well I had sorted out my normal Monday to Thursday routine, and how this was partly why I was doing so well with my treatment. Do too much and everything falls apart.

I went to bed at 8pm with my last sleeping tablet, feeling completely exhausted.

Saturday 19th May
Russ had set the alarm for 4am, as he was helping out at a race. My sleeping tablet didn't even get me that far! I wasn't convinced they had really helped.

After Russ left, I found myself on my own with an aching neck and back. My mouth felt awful, and I was sluggish and physically fragile. Maybe the sleeping tablet was still in my system. I decided to get up, have breakfast and take a long, hot bath, which I hoped would help with the aches and pains. I had planned to do a 10-mile run with Emma. Just before the run, I took some paracetamol. I expect at this point some people would have suggested I rest, but for me, this was a time to fight against the lethargy, and it was an approach that had worked for me so far.

When Emma arrived, the sleeping tablets had worn off and I was in a much better mood. The weather was gorgeous. We had the most enjoyable run around a familiar route. By the last few miles, my legs were struggling, but as always, the run had made me feel much better and so much more normal.

Soon after, my back and neck still ached, and I wondered if it was from over doing it at the gym. There was that familiar, uncomfortable sensation in my mouth that made it difficult to eat anything too hot. I was used to it now, so I didn't pay too much attention to it.

I had a second bath, did a few chores and lay on the sofa for a while. I was finding it difficult to warm up and swung easily from hot to cold. I checked my temperature, and it was OK.

I took some paracetamol before bed to try and combat my headache. Despite the weather being warm, I still felt cold. I managed to sleep until about 2am, when I found that I was sweating profusely and had to remove all the extra layers I had needed earlier. I then began to get cold and needed to wrap up again. Finally, I went downstairs to refill my hot water bottle, and I spent the rest of the evening lying on the sofa with the TV on. My temperature was a little high, but I had convinced myself that it was just from overdressing and then getting too hot and overcompensating.

Sunday 20th May

Despite the lack of sleep and temperature fluctuations, I stubbornly went out for a run. I decided to do the same 10-mile route as yesterday. This was probably a bit too far, but the weather was gorgeous and there was no rush. I walked up the first hill and then started a slow jog. I found it really hard to run. I had felt like this before, but for the first time since beginning treatment, I now had to continue with a walk. If I needed to walk the whole way, I was going to be out a long time, and I wasn't appropriately dressed for a stroll. After three miles, I decided to turn round and walk back home. I couldn't explain why I was unable to run. My legs just wouldn't work. I'd known this day was potentially coming, and I accepted the situation. I told myself that as long as I got myself out then that was fine. I also found my knees ached a little bit. Perhaps this was to do with the joint aches the nurse had described to me. I remembered that she had not been too concerned about them.

I was cold when I got home so I ran a bath. But no matter how hot I ran the water, it wasn't enough to warm me through. Russ made me a cup of tea, but as my mouth still felt awful, I only managed a few sips. I had to wrap myself up in a towel and get under the bedsheets with a hot water bottle to get warm before I could bring myself to get dressed. I measured my temperature, and it was just under 38C, but this was after being in a hot bath, so I decided that maybe it was a false reading.

I rang the hospital's 24-hour helpline for some advice. They asked me to take my temperature again. It was 38C. They asked me questions about other symptoms, but apart from feeling fluey there was nothing else to add. Despite this, I was told to come into the hospital immediately and to bring an overnight bag in case I had to stay in.

Upon arrival, the nurse asked me a few questions and retook my temperature. By their reading, it was 37.8C. She put a cannula in my arm. I was usually OK with this, but as I felt queasy, I had to lie down on the bed and look away. My blood pressure was fine. She asked me if I had been drinking enough. It was possible that I hadn't, as even water didn't taste particularly nice.

I was given antibiotics by IV, and my bloods were taken to find out if I was neutropenic. I was also asked to give a urine sample, but it was hours before I had drunk enough to get the urge to do this. I was clearly dehydrated, which probably explained the headache. The sweating in bed at night wouldn't have helped either.

The doctor visited a few hours later and told me I would need to stay in overnight. Any follow up would depend on my blood results. Fortunately, these came back OK, which meant I wasn't neutropenic. I was given fluids by IV to deal with my dehydration and a sleeping tablet to help me get some rest. I had a second IV of antibiotics in the evening and a third the following morning. The sleeping tablet knocked me out from 11pm until about 3am, when I woke up feeling exceptionally cold.

Monday 21st May
The oncology consultant came to determine whether I could be discharged. She was happy that my blood levels were good but ordered some extra antibiotics that I could take home with me, just in case I was still fighting something off. I mentioned that despite my temperature stabilising, I was still going from hot to cold during the night. Apparently, this was another common symptom of the docetaxel that I had not been warned about.

I felt well enough to walk the short distance home from the hospital. However, this was not as easy as I had expected it to be. The slight hill proved to be an effort.

I got home and lay on the sofa under a blanket. I did not even feel well enough to unpack my overnight bag. My aches and pains were getting worse. I didn't want to move from the sofa. At 2pm, I rang Russ feeling really sorry for myself and asking when he would be back. This was the first time I had felt the need to have him at home with me. I took a couple more paracetamols and eventually went up to bed. My body ached so much that I found it hard to even walk up the stairs. I relaxed on the bed and the pain eventually subsided.

I googled the side effects of docetaxel and found lots of comments from people who found the FEC treatment fine but the docetaxel far worse. Some described it as feeling like you'd been hit by a bus. Right now, I could relate to that. Also, many commented on how much worse their mouths were, and that they had found drinking water difficult. So, it wasn't just me, then. I read suggestions on what to eat whilst dealing with a sore mouth. Porridge was a top recommendation. I figured this was because as everything now tasted slimy, if you ate something you expected to taste slimy, it wouldn't seem so bad.

When the painkillers wore off, the aches and pains returned with a vengeance. I took a hot bath and then rang the breast care nurse. She advised me to try co-codamol, which has a longer lasting effect, and to take ibuprofen in between. We had both at home, so I took the co-codamol.

I messaged Sarah to tell her I had been in hospital. Back when she was on chemotherapy, she had been admitted on the same day in the cycle. She said her joint pain was so bad she couldn't get off the floor. She hadn't been told she could take painkillers. I couldn't imagine how awful that must have been, as the medication provided a great temporary relief. I asked her about the hot and cold flushes, and she said she had those too but had forgotten about them, which is why she hadn't mentioned them to me previously. She said the joint pain did subside, and based on her experience, I only had a couple of days of this to go.

I knew the co-codamol wouldn't get me through the night, so I took more with me upstairs and placed them on the floor by the bed. I also kept a bottle of water to drink if I woke up in the night. I put on loads of clothes, which I stripped off in layers as I became too hot and left within reach. During the night, I became cold again, but my body ached so much I couldn't even bring myself to get out of bed to get the painkillers or the warm clothes that were next to me. I knew I needed them, but I couldn't bear the thought of becoming even colder after emerging from the covers. Russ was in bed next to me, but I didn't want to wake him. I tried to get back to sleep, but it took ages because I was so cold. I needed to warm up my hot water bottle again, but I still didn't want to move. At 4am, I finally took some tablets and forced myself to go downstairs and lay on the sofa. I felt OK once the painkillers started to work.

The following morning was beautiful, so I decided to go out for a walk. I tried to run but it was impossible. I can't explain why. As I walked back towards the car, the painkillers started to wear off and my joints began to ache, particularly my hips. By the time I reached my vehicle, I was hunched over in pain. As soon as I got home, I took some more painkillers and had a warm bath, which helped. That night was another one swinging from too hot to too cold, which meant I also disrupted Russ's sleep. He had his 145-mile Grand Union Canal Race (running from Birmingham to London) coming up at the weekend, so I wasn't helping him much with his race preparation. My symptoms continued throughout the next day and night.

Thursday 24th May

As per usual, I woke up in the early hours. I felt really hot and lay there unable to bring myself to get up. I wasn't lethargic, I just didn't feel right. An hour later, I finally managed to make my way downstairs and take my temperature. It was 38.5C, higher than it had ever been! I couldn't understand it. I was still on antibiotics, so by rights I should be beginning to feel better.

I waited half an hour and took my temperature again. It was 38.6C. I started to get distressed and panicky, and I told Russ that I needed to go back to the hospital.

When I arrived, my temperature was taken, and I had to go through the whole process of being put on antibiotics and having tests carried out on my blood to try and identify the source of the infection.

My neutrophils were still fine, but my infection marker was raised again, so the registrar decided to send me for a chest X-ray to try and identify the source. The decision was made to admit me again. I was convinced they wouldn't let me out so quickly this time.

Russ was due to go to Birmingham the following afternoon in preparation for his race the next day. He didn't want to go while I was in hospital, but I insisted and said I would be fine. While he popped home for a couple of hours, I continued to swing from being too cold to too hot. My temperature was 38C. The nurse was not too concerned and gave me a couple of paracetamols, saying that it took time for the antibiotics to work. When Russ returned later that afternoon, I reiterated that he should go to Birmingham. It was part of his preparation for the Spartathlon race in September, and in my eyes, it was a vital piece of his training.

My temperature seemed to settle down a little through the night, and after my 11pm antibiotics, I took a sleeping tablet, which knocked me out until 3am. I then woke up with a massive pain in my side. I had lain in the same position for four straight hours. This was one of the downsides of a medication-induced sleep.

Friday 25th May
The veins in my right arm looked a mess, and the constant cannulas and blood tests were beginning to distress me. I discussed having a PICC line with the nurse. She told me to talk to the doctor when he came round. Events were beginning to drag me down, and I was emotionally and physically drained.

Russ had reluctantly agreed to go to Birmingham. He was not

convinced it was the right choice, but it was what I wanted him to do. He visited me in hospital at midday, at the same time as the doctor. I was now in good spirits and itching to get out, even though I didn't expect to be discharged any time soon. The doctor had decided that I did not have an infection and was hypersensitive to the docetaxel, which would also cause my infection markers to rise. He was very calm about it. He told me that I needed to explain what had happened to my consultant on my next appointment. He could give me an injection that would minimise my side effects. I wasn't keen on taking yet more medication, but I accepted that I didn't really have a choice. The doctor also said that since I was having adjuvant chemotherapy (treatment following surgery rather than before it), I could also discuss with the consultant a reduction in my dose. I was keen to do this, as it was exactly what had been done for Sarah. I didn't want a repeat of how I'd been feeling for the last week. The doctor said that if I developed a high temperature, I should still ring the 24-hour helpline. I would be admitted and given antibiotics again regardless. They would not take the risk of me having an infection. While he could not guarantee that a reduction in dose would decrease my side effects, I was still hopeful that this would help.

I asked the doctor about having a PICC line fitted, and he replied, 'You've only got two more cycles to go, I wouldn't worry.' I took his advice and hoped he was right. My poor arm had endured enough needle damage recently. I hoped it would recover enough to cope with what was to come.

I was now going to be at home while Russ went to Birmingham. I reassured him that I would be fine. If needed, there were plenty of people I could ring at any time of the day or night.

That evening, I was in bed by 8pm. At 9pm, I woke up drenched in sweat. My bed clothes were soaked, and it was as if someone had poured water over my head. I had never experienced anything like it.

Chapter 6 – Cycle 4

It was like an extreme menopausal hot flush. I settled down again but had another hot sweat at 10pm. It was just as bad, and as my sheets were drenched once again, I decided to get up and watch television for a while. I went back to bed at midnight and managed to sleep for four hours with no further incidents.

Saturday 26th May

I managed to speak to Russ before his race began at 6am. He had made it to the starting line and was in good spirits. I was so relieved. As I got up, I was slow and deliberate about everything I did, as I was still feeling fragile. I decided to have a bath, as I thought this might help me feel better.

My friend Amy had originally planned to take me to watch some of Russ's race, but I had cancelled while in hospital and she had made alternative arrangements. As Russ had taken the car, I decided to go online to hire one, though I was still not feeling well. It was a bank holiday weekend, and unsurprisingly, nothing was available. Deep down, I knew it wouldn't be sensible to go on a road trip right now. I sat in the lounge deeply disappointed that I was no longer able to support my husband and broke into uncontrollable tears. I knew this had been a long time coming, as all the stresses of the last week hit me. I cried harder than at any time previously.

To help me feel better, I decided to go for a short walk. On the way back, I received a text from my friend Julie. She suggested I could go up to Birmingham the following day with her husband, Iaan. She had been planning to go but was sure Russ would prefer to see me. Besides, she was only going to keep Iaan company, and she was happy to forfeit a day waiting in the car or hanging around the canal. I was overwhelmed by her offer and broke into tears again.

I continued to receive regular updates from friends and crew on Russ's progress. Late in the afternoon, he even managed to ring me while running, which was something I had not expected. He had already heard the news that I would be coming up after all. He was in good spirits, and everything so far was going to plan. He was at just over 50 miles, and his first running buddy, Tony, would be with him from 65 miles until about 87 miles, when his other friend, Rob, would take over to accompany him through the night. Tony would run with him again the following morning.

Sunday 27th May

Early the next morning, Russ managed to call me again. He described the amazing thunderstorms he had witnessed through the night. He was still in good spirits, but he was now a little behind schedule. The weather conditions had slowed him down.

I was feeling better than yesterday. I hadn't had a great night's sleep, but it was nowhere near as bad as what I had been dealing with lately. Iaan picked me up at noon and we drove down to meet Russ's crew at 127.5 miles. Russ had ONLY 17.5 miles to go. For him, this was an eternity. His blisters were causing him great discomfort. They had also altered his running gait, which meant he had back problems and a significant lean to one side. He was finding it almost impossible to run. After seeing him at a checkpoint, we planned to meet up with him again at the next one, in 5.5 miles. This was next to a pub, so we could get a drink and watch the other runners coming through. They had clearly been affected by the heat and were struggling to run. On top of this, they had been awake since 6am the previous morning, having run through a horrendous thunderstorm. Sleep deprived, undernourished, exhausted and now in blazing sunshine, it was no wonder they were trudging the last few miles. I was extremely jealous that I wasn't there with them. This is what ultra runners can expect to go through, and the ability to overcome these challenges is what makes reaching the finish line all the sweeter. I couldn't wait to get my entry in for next year! Many people don't understand why we want to put ourselves through such discomfort, but the sense of achievement after managing to overcome such adversity is significant.

We travelled to the next checkpoint six miles away and waited for Russ and his buddy, Tony, to arrive. Based on his pace, it looked like he was now walking, so we were expecting him in an hour and a half or so. I decided to walk up the canal in the opposite direction. His planned 4pm finish time was no longer achievable. The weather was gorgeous, for walkers at least. I used the opportunity to stroll a couple of pleasant miles in the sunshine. I had factor 50 on, just as my nurse had advised. When I finally saw Russ with his buddy, his back was so painful he was walking with a stoop and leaning to the left, towards the canal. It was going to be a long, painful trudge to the finish line.

We said goodbye to Russ for the last time. Next time we saw him would be at the finish six miles further along the canal. We were in for an extended wait. I was conscious of all the germs due to the mingling crowds of runners and supporters standing around the finish line, so I decided to walk up the canal again to see Russ come through with Tony. I finally saw him when he had just under two miles to go. Occasionally, he tried to run, but his lean to the left meant he was at risk of falling into the canal, and Tony had to keep putting his arm out to stop this happening. As he continued the last few yards to the finishing line, he couldn't run in a straight line.

Russ finished in 39 hours and 40 minutes. The race took him more than four hours longer than planned, but with half the runners having dropped out before the finish, he could be proud to have dug deep and reached the end, despite all the issues he had faced. Hopefully, he had also learned a lot of lessons for Spartathlon, where he had 154 miles to complete in under 36 hours, and with a mountain to climb at 100 miles!

We left Little Venice, in Paddington, not long after 10pm. This was a lot later than we had originally anticipated, but the job was done. I had survived the day out without too much difficulty. I was clearly more fragile than I would normally be at this time in my cycle, but I had spent most of the day sitting around, so altogether, it had not been too stressful for me.

Monday 28th May
In the morning, I tried my run from the back of my house. It started with a hill, so I walked this, and I found that my breathing was laboured even then. When I got on the flat, I inexplicably couldn't run for more than a few seconds. The weather was good, and the views were great, so I continued to walk the route.

Russ was off work over the next two days to recover from his race. I stuck to my morning running routine but continued to find it difficult. The merest breeze brought me to a standstill. It felt like such hard work, but yet again, I couldn't explain what was preventing me. My breath was laboured, but not like it was when I was running hard. My legs didn't ache, but even so, they just did not seem to work. I found myself crying tears of frustration. It felt like the chemotherapy had finally beaten me. It took a while for me to compose myself again, but eventually, I got my head straight and reminded myself how I had vowed that if I couldn't run, I would walk instead. Finally, on my fourth cycle, this was where I was at. So, I proceeded to walk the entire route. I would put in the odd 30-second shuffle, but that was all I could manage. I stuck to the same route over the following days and gave myself a target to improve my time each day by running a little more than before. Giving myself a focus kept me moving forward and continued to provide me with a little control over what was happening.

I found I was beginning to sleep well through the night. On top of this, I also needed a decent nap in the day. The fatigue was having a more significant effect on me. Despite all this, I was determined to get in some exercise. I believed it would help not hinder the tiredness. Even a walk was better than nothing.

Saturday 2nd June
On Saturday morning, Russ and I were up at 4am to make the long drive to Manchester to see his son Dan, Dan's partner, and their two children, who were four and a half, and 11 months old. It was an early start for two reasons. One, to miss the horrendous traffic queues you would get at any other time of the day, and two, so that we could do the Bramhall Parkrun again.

It was a hilly route, so I was fully expecting to do some walking. With other runners around me, I pushed harder than I would have done had I been running on my own. Despite struggling to catch my breath at times, I only had to walk twice along the whole route. It wasn't fast, but it was still better than I had expected. I couldn't run anywhere near as fast as I used to, but I was able to accept this and be happy doing what I could do. Despite being slower, I felt this was keeping my fitness levels up ready for when I could return to running properly.

We stayed in a hotel overnight and spent the rest of the time with family. It was obvious that I was more tired than usual. I was sleeping most of the day and still slept heavily at night. I savoured the sleep, as I knew that in a few days' time, it would be back to the steroids and no decent rest for at least a week.

Monday 4th June
I had my regular pre-chemotherapy appointment with my consultant. I discussed the side effects that I'd experienced and my recent admission to hospital. She felt the hypersensitivity regime would not be appropriate for me, as this was for people who had side effects immediately following the injection, and mine had come on a few

days later. She decided to reduce the chemotherapy dose by 25%. I was relieved to hear this, as this approach had worked so well for Sarah. We also discussed the side effects from the increased steroids. As I didn't have any fluid retention issues, she agreed to halve the dose. This was also a great relief. Even this amount would keep me awake, but hopefully, I wouldn't have the added mood swings and anxiety issues. Finally, she prescribed more sleeping tablets in case I felt I needed them.

Chapter 7
Cycle 5 / Purbrook Ladies 5

Wednesday 6th June

Attending my fifth chemotherapy session made me feel like I had turned a corner and was on the home straight. There was still some way to go, but perhaps the worst was now over. It was also good to know that the next time I went for treatment would be my last. My blood levels were generally OK, but my haemoglobin levels had dropped further – to 106. The consultant wasn't worried about the number, but to some degree, it would still affect how I felt when I exercised.

On the morning before my appointment, I still managed to go out for a run, and I continued to try and run each day, but now I had to walk the hills, and even on the flat I would need to stop and walk now and then. I tried to keep upbeat about it. I was still running most of the time. That was good enough for now.

Sunday 10th June

A few months ago, I decided to enter the Purbrook Ladies 5. It is a small, local, friendly event for women of all levels. There is no cut off, so it's fine to walk the whole route if you want to.

When I entered the race, I had no idea whether it would be possible for me to complete it, but I figured that at least I'd be able to finish it by walking. This was one of the challenges I had set to motivate myself to keep up with my exercise.

As I had been feeling a little unwell in the days leading up to the event, I had emailed the event organisers and asked if my friend,

Angie, could run with me as a support runner. This was in case I did not feel well at any time, and she could look after me rather than the race organisers having to. They kindly agreed to this.

When the morning came, however, I was not certain that I would even make the starting line. My temperature had been up in the night, and I had woken up with a headache and felt a little nauseous, which was generally unlike me. After rising early and putting on my running gear, I took a paracetamol and an anti-sickness tablet and went back to bed for a while to see if the sick feeling would pass.

I began to feel a little better and decided to give the race a go. Angie cycled down to meet me, and we agreed to go for a 10-minute mile, with possible walking up the hills. I didn't expect I would be able to run the whole way.

It was a lovely sunny day and I decided to wear my sun cap rather than a buff. We started near the middle of the pack, and I found myself running my first mile in nine minutes. Faster than I had planned but there had been a couple of downhill sections. It wasn't easy but I'd coped so far. It did feel more like a race though, and I was really pleased to find that I was able to get up the hills without walking. With a mile to go, I passed Russ marshalling on one of the last hills. By that point, I was finding it really tough going, but I didn't want to slow down or walk. We got through the last mile with Angie encouraging me, but at the same time checking I was OK and wasn't overdoing it, even though I was clearly struggling. We pushed up the last hill before the final turn into the finish and then sprinted together to the line. It was only five miles, but it felt like a great deal more to me.

We received our goody bags and medals and sat on the grass to recover. The race organisers asked if I minded the local newspaper taking a picture of us, and I agreed to this together with a quick interview, even feeling confident enough to remove my running cap for the picture. I hoped I might help others by showing that it was possible to continue to exercise through chemotherapy. The article came out later in the week in the Portsmouth News.

The sense of wellbeing and achievement I felt after the event was immense. I had finished much faster than expected, and I hadn't had to walk any of the hills. I began to believe that despite being on my fifth chemotherapy cycle, perhaps I was beginning to recover from the effects of the fourth one, when I had had such a bad reaction. Perhaps I could get back to the longer mileage training that I had been doing at the beginning of my chemotherapy. I relaxed for the rest of the day and felt more confident about getting to the point where I could prepare sufficiently to attempt the Autumn 100 in October.

Saturday 16th June
I managed to continue with my running every day throughout the week. I was still finding it more difficult, though, and my legs ached a lot. By the weekend I felt confident enough to tackle nine miles. I travelled down to Southsea to run along the seafront but found that running against any wind was impossible, and as I trudged along, I shed tears of frustration. Despite my earlier positivity about continuing to run, I now felt completely demoralised. It reminded me of how I felt when I had anaemia.

I experienced my first ever bout of anaemia back in 2006. I was taking a 14mg iron tablet every morning, so I didn't even consider that I could develop it. However, I had been taking an over-the-counter tablet with my morning cup of tea, which I didn't realise inhibited the iron absorption and made the tablet less effective. I found myself struggling with my running and had to pull out in the middle of a race. At only two miles in, I felt like I had run 20 miles already, and

I had no idea why. I also found myself feeling emotional and down and would cry easily. I felt that something was wrong, but I couldn't put my finger on it, so I went to the doctors for a blood test. When I got the results a week later, I cried with relief. Just knowing why made everything seem better. My haemoglobin level was at about 90, and it should have been at 120. I was given a prescription of 210mg of ferrous fumarate to take three times a day for a few months. I had a half marathon to do the following week. It was tough getting through it, but I no longer minded because I knew why I was struggling. Four to five weeks later, I felt I was getting back to my old self, and I was already beginning to get my running legs back. It no longer felt like I was running through treacle.

The tiredness I felt while running with anaemia was different to the usual feeling of getting out of breath. Your whole body feels like it doesn't have the energy to move forward. I can only liken it to the end of doing an ultra, when you have run out of energy and find it difficult to do more than a few steps at a time. You feel that you need to walk, even though you can't put your finger on why. Your muscles are worn out from constant use and all your internal energy resources are used up, which makes every single step a colossal effort. There is also mental fatigue from being on your feet for hours. Running with anaemia feels a lot like this. By likening the feeling to running an ultra, I was able to manage the feelings I was having so much better. I realised that I just needed to keep putting one foot in front of the other and eventually I would get there. This is what I continued to do.

I managed to get a telephone appointment with my GP. I was already taking two 210mg ferrous sulphate tablets a day, and he suggested increasing this to three per day. The following week, I continued to try and run. Although it was still a struggle, I found that going off road on a hilly trail was more enjoyable than a flat road run. Having hills gave me an excuse for a walk break, and I was lifted up rather than feeling downhearted about the difficulties I was experiencing.

I had also noticed that my eyes and nose would run while I was out. I was aware that my lack of hair could be causing this, or it could just be high pollen levels. However, I hadn't previously encountered this problem. As soon as I stopped running it would go away. Continually wiping my eyes and nose as I ran was frustrating, and they gradually became sorer.

Friday 21st June
I had an appointment with my radiotherapy consultant, who explained how there was a one in four chance of the breast cancer reoccurring if I chose not to have the radiotherapy treatment. As four of my lymph nodes had been found to contain cancer cells, I would also require radiotherapy treatment to the lymph nodes in my neck. All those under my left armpit had now been removed. I expressed my concerns about the risk to my heart. He explained that current statistics estimate that undergoing radiotherapy increases the risk of having a heart attack by two to three percent. However, it would be clearer to see the extent to which the heart would be in the treatment field following my CT scan, which would be in about a week's time. I would hear about this soon via an appointment letter. Once the treatment plan was made, I would have an opportunity to talk it through at another appointment.

I asked about exercising if I developed skin damage. The recommendation was to regularly use E45 cream on the area, as it would get dry and resemble sunburn. Generally, this would be manageable, but in some cases, it could become very sore, and the skin may break and leak fluid. At this point, it might not be possible to run, as I wouldn't be able to wear any clothes that were tight on my skin, but everything would settle down within two to four weeks.

The consultant explained that my problems with anaemia would not be worsened by the radiotherapy. He said it wasn't clear why people experience fatigue, but the main theory is that it occurs as the body tries to repair itself from the cell damage. He did not feel I should be too concerned about it.

The treatment was likely to start close to three weeks after my last chemotherapy cycle. I asked for morning appointments so that I could start going to work in the afternoons to get myself gradually used to being there, without overdoing it. Once the chemotherapy was over, I would no longer have such a risk of infection.

Saturday 22nd June
For my final weekend prior to chemotherapy, I went for a 15-mile run around Portsea Island, but I found that I couldn't run for more than a few minutes at a time, despite this being when I should be feeling at my best. The continuing cycle of having poison injected into my body before everything had time to fully recover was taking its toll. The nurse's prediction that everything would get worse was now evident. After all my body had been through these last few months, I couldn't expect to be feeling perfectly OK. After a few more attempts at run/walking, I finally decided to walk the rest of the route. It took over four hours, and afterwards, I felt exhausted for the rest of the day.

At this point, I did consider having a break from running. Perhaps my body needed a complete rest, but at the same time, I had been told that exercise helped with the fatigue, and that I should do it when I could. I started to do more walking. The weather was gorgeous, so I had no issue with getting out regularly for a stroll, but as the time for my next treatment drew near, I found myself more able to run again. It was difficult to know from one day to another how I would feel. I just had to listen to my body and adjust my exercise accordingly. I now only had one more cycle to go.

Chapter 7 – Cycle 5 / Purbrook Ladies 5

Monday 25th June

I had my pre-chemotherapy appointment with my consultant, who explained that everything would remain the same with this next cycle, including the 25% lower dose. I would be given some tamoxifen tablets when I came for my next round of chemotherapy, and I would need to start taking these approximately three weeks after my final treatment. Tamoxifen is designed to stop oestrogen production and would bring on an early menopause if I was not already at this stage. I had read up on the side effects: hot flushes, night sweats, sleep disturbance, mood changes and headaches. I expressed my concerns, but the consultant told me not to worry about it and just see how I got on. She gave me another blood form so I could have an additional test of my hormone levels to see if I was pre-menopausal or had reached the menopause. If pre-menopausal, I would need additional monthly injections to prevent my ovaries from working. She booked an appointment for two to three months' time to review this. No further thrice-weekly, pre-chemo appointments needed to be booked in this time. The end was in sight.

Chapter 8
Cycle 6 / North Downs Half Marathon

Wednesday 27th June

After a short, interrupted sleep (thank you, steroids) and a five-mile run from the back of my house, I went for my CT-treatment planning appointment. I was familiar with the radiotherapy department's CT scanner, as I had carried out safety checks on it, but it felt different to be present as a patient. I was taken into the relevant room, asked some questions and then asked to remove the top half of my clothing behind some curtains. When ready, I was helped onto the CT scanning table. My arms were placed above my head and rested in a specially designed contraption. I was already aware of what was going to happen from an earlier visit as part of my job, and from the leaflets I had been given. Two radiographers worked in well-practised unison to ensure I was positioned exactly where I needed to be. Three small tattoo marks were inscribed on my skin so that I could be positioned in the same way again when I returned for my actual treatment in a few weeks' time.

I had one scan whilst breathing normally, and then the radiographer went through the breath hold technique with me, which I practised a couple of times. When I had the radiotherapy treatment, I would take a deep breath and hold it for up to 20 seconds while the scan was carried out. This would ensure my heart was moved further out of the treatment field. The radiographer explained that not all patients need to carry out the technique, as it depends on the natural position of the heart.

I was given all my radiotherapy treatment dates; fifteen in total. My last day was booked in for August 7th. I was surprised that the whole CT appointment had taken an hour.

I returned to the waiting room for my final chemotherapy appointment. A nurse came to fit my cannula. Unfortunately, she tried three times without success. Many of my veins were now damaged from previous chemotherapy appointments, and from the antibiotics that had been administered intravenously when I'd been unwell. A more experienced nurse came along and managed to set it up first time. Such a relief. At this last hurdle, I didn't want to end up with a PICC line.

I was given my standard medication but no steroids. It was great to know there would be no need to take them once my remaining two-day supply had been used up. I was also given a box of tamoxifen, with instructions to start taking them in four weeks' time. I was not looking forward to these at all. Five years of taking them to stop my oestrogen production, with possibly more side effects as a result. Despite the reassurances of my oncologist, it was something that concerned me.

My blood tests showed that my haemoglobin levels had gone up from 106 to 116, which I was really pleased about. The iron tablets appeared to be working. The rest of the treatment went according to plan, and as I left the day unit, I let out a cheer. I wasn't planning on coming back here again any time soon.

Thursday 28th June
As expected, thanks to the steroids I had very little sleep and was up by 4am. I went out for a run from the back of the house. Again, I felt good, as the side effects of the chemotherapy had not yet kicked in. I could run up hills without feeling like my batteries had been drained, as I had with the anaemia. Today didn't feel like that at all, and I

had a good session. I knew it would be two weeks or so before I felt anything close to this good again.

Saturday 30th June
By the weekend, I no longer felt strong. I found the docetaxel treatment had affected me more than the FEC, and also far earlier in the cycle. Russ was doing the Southsea Parkrun, so I decided I would do it too and just see how I got on. The mile run to the start became a walk, and I doubted I would be able to break into a run. However, I ended up having some friends with me, and we all ran together. Though hard, it was much easier doing it with other people while chatting as we went (although there wasn't much chatting from me!). I took my buff off while sitting in the shade having a coffee. I was aware of a little bit of fluff on my head now. Hopefully, this would thicken and grow rather than fall out. I would just have to wait and see.

I knew the next week would be difficult, but I realised how lucky I was to have so many friends who would run and walk with me and help get me through the tough times when I needed it. This was to be the last week of feeling rough, and from the following weekend it would be onwards and upwards. I was so looking forward to being back to my old self.

Sunday 1st July
I met my friend Len for a run/walk around Queen Elizabeth Country Park. Previously, we had met there regularly for a run with our mutual friends, Angie and Emma Louise, while my dad sat in the café. Len was happy to do whatever pace I needed. It was more of a social catch up than anything. Len was 70, but he still managed to get out most mornings for a run with friends or a trip to the gym. As we progressed, I found I could run a little more. My body seemed to

Chapter 8 – Cycle 6 / North Downs Half Marathon

grow accustomed to it. Even though I was still running quite slow and feeling out of breath, I managed to push myself to tackle a few small inclines. I finished the run with a massive sense of achievement and, as always, I felt so much better than I had done before I started.

My side effects so far were all manageable, and as I would have expected at this stage. My muscles were aching in my back, and I think this was mainly due to the chemotherapy. The skin was peeling from my feet, which were also a bit numb, but I was now used to this. My mouth felt a little weird and some foods tasted different, but again, I was used to it, so it didn't generally affect what I ate anymore. I was finding now that my fingernails hurt. It wasn't the pads of my fingers but the very ends of my nails, which made it difficult to type. I had felt this a little on the previous cycle, but it was worse this time. It was still manageable, but I wondered if it was the symptom that people experienced before their nails fell out. I would have to wait and see. As I had been advised, I was still religiously painting my nails with dark nail varnish, to try and limit any damage.

One year ago, at this exact point in time, I had just finished the Thames Ring 250. Somehow, now felt like the right time to finally post something on Facebook. This was a very similar point to when Sarah had written her first post, and I now understood her timing completely. She had said that the end of her sixth chemotherapy session was liberating, but at the time I hadn't really understood. I hadn't felt it would all be over until I got past the side effects, but this wasn't the case. I did feel liberated. I uploaded a picture of me alongside the Thames with only one mile left to go, together with a video of the finish, and then a picture with the words, 'You must do the things you think you cannot do.' I then wrote:

One year ago today, I finished the Thames Ring 250. There were times when I thought I wouldn't even make it to the start line, but

I did, and now I look back and know that it was the best decision I could ever have made. I have made memories that I cherish, which will live inside me forever.

One year on and I have finished my last chemotherapy cycle for breast cancer after surgery in January. There is just radiotherapy to go and five years of drugs, but I can now see light at the end of the tunnel, and I am busy hatching my next challenges.

Do the things that scare you a bit (or a lot!). Look back with no regrets and live your life. Don't let it pass you by thinking, *I wish I had done that*. Do it now!

Wednesday 4th July

Perhaps I had been a little hasty in my optimism about my side effects on this cycle. I woke up early (due to the steroids, no doubt), feeling groggy and not particularly well. I questioned whether it was a good idea to go out for a longer run when it was now day eight in the cycle. I took a paracetamol for the grogginess and a while later took an anti-sickness tablet, as I was feeling a little queasy. Half an hour later, I found that I had a couple of episodes of diarrhoea, something that had previously tended to happen much later in my cycle. I took the medication prescribed for it and administered my filgrastim injection, noting with relief that after this, I only had one more to go.

After doing everything I could to combat the nausea, I finally decided that I would attempt the trail run I had planned. However, as soon as I started to run, I could tell my legs were not really up to it. I found that I had to run/walk even the flat parts. This route was quite undulating, so I would walk the uphill, run/walk the flat and then run downhill. My eyes and nose were streaming. My consultant believed these symptoms were related to the chemotherapy. This made sense, and I figured that in a week or so it would settle down. Yet another side effect to deal with.

Chapter 8 – Cycle 6 / North Downs Half Marathon

I had booked a GP appointment to discuss how I would return to work. I explained my plan to go in for a couple of hours in the afternoons whilst on radiotherapy, followed by a phased return from mid-August. She told me that radiotherapy could cause extreme tiredness and that I might find the plan difficult to execute. I explained that I was doing exercise in the mornings and trying to put my health first, but that I wanted to go back and help at work. I then received a lecture.

'Of course you should put your health first at this time,' said the GP. 'What good will you be to anyone if you are dead?'

I suppose this was her shock tactic to stop me trying to plan my return to work too rigidly. She wrote me out another note for the following two months, stating that I may be fit for work but needed flexibility regarding the hours and location. I said that my infection risk would be less now I was on the radiotherapy, but she disagreed and suggested I was still very vulnerable, which needed to be taken into account.

Saturday 8th July
A few months ago, I entered the North Downs Half Marathon in preparation for upping my training for the Autumn 100. It was yet another goal to aim for.

Russ and I drove to the start near Reigate. It was going to reach 30 degrees, and I considered whether to take a backpack to hold my own water. In the end, I decided against carrying the extra weight and would rely on the checkpoints to rehydrate. I admitted to Russ how nervous I felt. I had seven hours to complete the route, so I could walk the whole way if I wanted to, but my aim was to run as much as possible and see how I coped.

I set off near the back of the group and ran at a slow, steady pace, hoping I could keep this up both on the outward and return journey.

The route went down Reigate Hill, at just over two miles, before snaking along the North Downs route to Box Hill, where you went up steep steps to reach a viewpoint before turning around and heading back down again.

I found I could run all the flats and downhills, but I didn't have the energy to run up any of the hills. At least my fitness was good enough to allow me to march up the steep ones, and while hiking, I even managed to overtake a few runners.

I was thrilled to finish the race in just over two and a half hours. This wasn't fast by any means, but a significant achievement for me just 11 days after my final chemotherapy treatment. I'd worked my way through a whole pack of tissues to deal with my streaming eyes and nose, but at least I'd come prepared.

Having surmounted a very significant hurdle, I could see me moving forward with my training for the Autumn 100. I had got through my last bad week post chemotherapy, and there would be no more. It felt like a huge weight had been lifted. I'd also run much better than I had expected to, and this reminded me of how it can be in an ultra. When you run a 100-mile race, you inevitably go through bad patches. At 60 miles, you can feel completely exhausted, yet you have another 40 to go and can't see how you can finish. Somehow, you continue to push yourself forwards. You may be slower and barely able to run at times, but you keep going. Then you finally get closer to the end, muster some energy from somewhere and find yourself running again for the very last part of your race. It felt like that during the chemotherapy. When I was halfway through, the bad weeks were much harder to deal with, as I knew there was still more to come. But now that I had undergone my final one, I could cope with it better. This demonstrated how hard the mental battle had been in the middle of chemotherapy, and how having the right attitude had played a significant role in how I had got through it. Previously, I had

Chapter 8 – Cycle 6 / North Downs Half Marathon

felt that a positive mental attitude wouldn't have any bearing on how the treatment affected me, but looking back, I am convinced that it does impact how quickly you recover from each cycle. Being fit is a factor, but being positive is also important.

During the week, I followed a similar pattern of a walk on Monday followed by a run on Tuesday, Wednesday and Thursday. While following similar routes to my previous runs, I could tell that I was beginning to feel better.

Saturday 14th July
I had put together a training plan for the Autumn 100, and a 15-mile run round Portsea Island was my target for the weekend. Russ also had 15 miles to do that morning, so we agreed to start together. If it went well, I would feel more positive about the continuation of my training plan. If it didn't, I would need to have a rethink. Despite my concerns, everything went smoothly. It was a while since I had been able to run with Russ, so doing so felt like a huge achievement.

In the afternoon, we joined our friends Russ and Sarah at the local leisure centre. Sarah was walking and running around the athletics track for 24 hours to raise money for a child with cancer. We had sponsored her, and we wanted to show her our support. It seemed like a great event. Tents and gazebos had been set up on the green in the middle of the track for the participants to rest, and there was loud music playing throughout, together with regular supportive announcements. Most people were wearing light blue T-shirts bearing the statement, 'Together we are stronger – stand up to cancer.' Others were wearing purple tops and accessories. Sarah explained that those people were cancer survivors, and at the start of the event and for every hour during it, they would walk around the track together while everyone else stood to one side. I found it strange to think that I was a cancer survivor now. I had noticed how there were online groups for people who had finished their cancer treatment but were struggling to get back to their normal life. They felt the cancer had changed them forever, and in ways that other people couldn't comprehend. I understood why people would need the support of these networks, but I felt mentally ready to get back to my normal life and had no such concerns. I looked at the people walking around in purple, and despite it being clear from my lack of hair that I was a recent survivor myself, I knew I did not want to be seen as one in the future. All the same, it was significant to see so many supporters out raising money, and how many people had previously had cancer or were still fighting it. I was reminded how cancer touches almost everyone's life in some way.

Monday 16th July
Three weeks on since my last chemotherapy session, I agreed to go into work for the afternoon. It was to be the first time since mid-March that I would go into the office in my work clothes. Getting ready felt strange, and I found it took me longer than normal to get everything sorted. The weather was still very warm thanks to a lengthy heatwave, and it seemed odd to be putting on trousers, socks and shoes when typically, I would be in shorts and a T-shirt. My hair was clearly beginning to grow, but it was still in a downy, short, thin layer, so I put on one of my headscarves.

After returning home from the office, I felt unexpectedly tired. Reintroducing work into my daily routine had clearly had an effect, but it was something I'd assumed I would take in my stride. I would continue as planned after starting my radiotherapy treatment and see how I got on.

Chapter 9
Radiotherapy

Wednesday 18th July

For my first radiotherapy treatment, I went to the main reception in Oncology – the same place where I'd gone for my chemotherapy appointments. This time, I waited until I was called by one of the radiographers.

As it was my first treatment, I was taken into a small consultation room and asked a few questions. I confirmed that I still wanted to go ahead and was shown the CT image, which revealed how my heart would be out of the treatment field if I used the breath hold technique. I was given a gown to wear, which was essentially a top with poppers at the front and along both shoulders. It was designed to be easy to undo and button back up before and after treatment. I was told I should take the top home and keep it for all my treatments, before returning it again when it was all over.

I was taken into one of the Linear Accelerator (Linac) treatment rooms. The room was very large, and the treatment table was located at the centre of it, with a huge empty space all around it. Although this would have been daunting for some people, I had already been in this room several times as a staff member, so it was a familiar environment. However, this didn't alter the fact that as a patient I still felt vulnerable, and I was keen to follow the instructions I was given without question or hesitation.

The radiographers moved quickly and efficiently, with an ease that demonstrated how routine this process was for them. The patient table was lowered so that I could easily get on it, before being raised to the correct height for treatment. My legs were positioned with my knees bent over a foam pad so that I wouldn't slip down the table accidentally, and my arms were raised above my head on either side and placed on dedicated arm holders to ensure they remained still and out of the way.

One of the radiographers asked me to take a breath and then hold it. While I was doing this, they drew a number of felt-tip marks on my skin to define the treatment field. The radiographers would be outside the room during the process, but they assured me they would be able to view me remotely the whole time. If I accidentally moved from the correct position or couldn't keep my breath hold, they would stop the treatment and either reposition me or get me to hold my breath again before continuing.

The treatment plan that had been prepared for me would determine the correct dose to be administered at the appropriate depth under my skin to kill the cells in the region where the tumour had been. Lead shields would be remotely placed in front of the radiation exit port to prevent other areas of my chest receiving unnecessary radiation. The total radiation dose would be high enough to cause damage to the outer skin. To reduce the level of damage, the whole dose is divided into 15 separate treatments (fractions), so that the skin has time to heal in between procedures. Patients generally experience some skin reddening after about 10 days, and the radiographers advised me to use a skin cream on the area each day to prevent it from becoming too dry. It might also feel sore and itchy. In some cases, the skin damage can be worse, which leads to it breaking and leaking fluid. I was assured this should all settle down two to four weeks after treatment.

Once all the marks had been made, the radiographers left the room and talked to me via an intercom. The large machine moved around me as they remotely set up the start position. I could see the collimators in the Linac head moving into position. The first two procedures only required a two-to-four-second breath hold, as my breast was positioned correctly in the treatment field. Once this was done, the radiographers returned and placed some measurement diodes on my skin. They explained how these would measure the actual dose to confirm that what they were giving me was the correct quantity of radiation. They then left the room again and began the treatment. Altogether, there were three treatments; two were from opposite sides of my breasts and the third was on my breastbone, above my left breast. This was designed to target the lymph nodes in my neck.

Although each treatment lasted about 15 seconds, the procedures combined meant that my arms had been above my head for approximately half an hour. My fingers were numb, and I was desperate to scratch an itch on my nose! It was such a relief when I was finally allowed to take my hands down. The poppers from my top were put back so that I could walk out of the treatment room. I changed back into my own clothes and that was it for the day. Day One was over, and I had 14 to go. My treatments were carried out Monday to Friday, with weekends off. In three weeks, it would all be over.

Sunday 22nd July
I had a marathon booked, but I was still feeling tired and sluggish and worried how I would manage. I had entered it some time ago. It was a lapped event where you could choose how many laps you did within a six-hour period. Russ was planning to do a marathon distance and keep up a 10-minute-mile pace throughout. This was part of his long-distance training for Spartathlon. I decided I would try and run with him.

The event was held at Stansted Park, which is only 20 minutes from home. It was a 3.8-mile out and back loop, with a checkpoint available at the end of each one. Each time you finished a loop, you collected a coloured wristband. We were planning on doing seven loops, which would mean just over a marathon. The route was slightly undulating and had a left and a right-hand bend in the middle, which would make the route a little more interesting.

We started a 10-minute-mile pace as planned. It was a little crowded for the first lap, but it thinned out over the second one, and even more so after the fourth. Many people had dropped out by the half-marathon distance. The weather was due to reach 30 degrees, but fortunately, a large proportion of the route was on paths through woods, which protected us from the sun. There was a three-quarter mile stretch where we were fully exposed to the sun's harsh rays, but most of the course was more comfortable. By the time we reached four loops, I felt more confident that I was going to get the next three done and complete the marathon distance. The inclines now felt a little harder, but we still managed to run them and stick rigidly to our pace goal. We just took a couple of minutes extra at the turnaround point to refuel.

With a final lap to go, I ran strong up the last incline. I thought about all the times, just a few weeks back, when I couldn't even get up an incline that was significantly smaller than the one I was climbing now. It was clear that my perseverance and stubbornness were paying off. I was glad I'd taken each day as it came and got out of the house for a run even when my body was telling me to stay at home and lie on the sofa, and even when that led to me crying because I didn't even have the energy to run on a flat road against a mild wind. Now I knew that it had all been worth it. My last marathon had been in February, and here I was only five months later managing to complete another one despite everything that I had been through.

Chapter 9 – Radiotherapy

We walked into the checkpoint/finish of our final loop. I felt the tears well up inside me. I was so pleased (not to mention relieved) to have achieved what I had set out to do. Once I had gathered myself and got my emotions in check, I sat on a camp chair and smiled with contentment with my medal round my neck.

It wasn't easy – it was a marathon after all – but it certainly wasn't as hard as it might have been. I strongly believe that running during my chemotherapy treatment gave me the mental strength to cope. I also believe that the running helped with my fatigue, which it would hopefully continue to do as I went through radiotherapy. I just had to keep a good balance and not overdo it.

Tuesday 24th July

I had arranged to take Russ to hospital with me, so that he could see what the radiotherapy treatment involved. The radiographers allowed him into the control room whilst I was having the procedure and explained the breath hold technique to him. It was good for me to share this experience with him, as I wanted him to understand what I was going through.

I also started to take the dreaded tamoxifen. I had decided to take it in the evening, as I had read that it could reduce its side-effects during the day.

Friday 27th July

Our friend Mich was doing the 145-mile Kennet and Avon Canal Race. Russ and I drove up to Bristol the day before with his girlfriend, Amy, so that we could support him on his adventure. It was a similar format to the GUCR event that Russ had entered earlier in the year.

At 6am, we watched Mich set off from Bristol on his non-stop run, which would eventually see him finishing in Little Venice, Paddington.

Russ, Amy and I were to follow the route and provide Mich with food and drink at pre-arranged points. We first met him at 20 miles and then saw him every four to six miles after that. The weather was not as hot as it had been in the week, when it had reached over 30 degrees, but it was still warm and humid. When Mich got to about 72 miles, Russ would run with him for 35, and when he reached the 116-mile mark, I was planning to run with him for 10.

However, I found myself really struggling as I walked along the canal and up a steep path at one of our meeting points. My legs felt heavy and fatigued. I had also spent most of the morning asleep in the car. I was concerned whether I would be able to run with Mich after all. The heaviness in my legs made it difficult to walk, let alone run. I had been feeling tired all week, which made training hard. Fortunately, as the day wore on, I began to feel more energetic.

Russ had a good 35-mile run with Mich, who was doing well despite the heat and wasn't wasting any time at checkpoints. Amy and I had met up with them through the night at various planned points and made them tea and biscuits or hot food such as pot noodles, pasta and porridge.

After Russ left Mich, he would have 14 miles to run on his own before I joined him. I had decided to only do 10 miles because I had already entered a run called the Midnight Marathon, which was due to start at 9pm on Saturday evening from Queen Elizabeth Country Park. By the time I started my buddying stint with Mich, it was already light. He continued to run with minimal walking, although he was slowing down a little. This was hardly surprising, as the temperature was increasing again as the sun rose and the clouds dissipated. Rather than leave Mich to run by himself, I ended up running 20 miles in total and left him with only nine to go. Russ would support him for the final six.

Chapter 9 – Radiotherapy

Meanwhile, Amy and I drove to the end of the route so we could cheer them on. Mich finished in second place overall, which was great to witness. After a short sit down, we drove home. I had to have a bath and get into bed for a few hours in preparation for the midnight marathon later that night.

I struggled to sleep, and I worried that perhaps I had bitten off more than I could chew, having already run 20 miles from 6am that morning. From 9pm, I was going to be running a hilly marathon along the South Downs Way in the dark. I knew it would be sensible to give the whole thing a miss, but being the stubborn person that I am, I still drove to Queen Elizabeth Country Park and set off at 9pm in the half-light for my overnight run, which would take me to Cocking and back. Even the first hill was a challenge, and it wasn't long before I found myself struggling to walk up all the hills. It took me longer to reach Harting Down than it had done on my training runs whilst on chemo. I knew it was going to be a long night and was thankful for the checkpoints en route, where I could rest and have some food and drink. I found every step hard going.

I arrived at the Cocking halfway checkpoint, which had a real party atmosphere and provided a refuge from the dark. I grabbed a large chocolate chip muffin and a cup of tea and, before I could give myself a chance to think about pulling out, I started walking slowly back up the hill that I had only just come down. It had taken me three hours to get here, and it was now midnight. It was going to take me at least another four hours to get back, and possibly longer if I walked the whole way.

Even walking up the hill was hard. I had taken on too much and I was tired due to having very little sleep the previous night whilst crewing for Mich. What had I been thinking? Someone from a nearby group of participants asked me how I was doing. They were walking the hills and running the downs and flats, and I managed to stick with them for a while. My legs were extremely tired. I knew I had overdone it, but I was committed now and determined to finish what I had started.

I trudged on, taking a cup of tea and some biscuits at the next checkpoint. I tried to be more positive about the experience and just enjoy being out on the Downs in the middle of the night. When I reached more familiar territory after Harting Down, I ran whenever I could and enjoyed the last long downhill stretch to the finish. I told myself that I had better get used to feeling like this and accept it, as it wasn't going to be any easier on the day of the Autumn 100 in October. If I had any hope of completing the race, this really was essential training.

Thursday 2nd August
I had radiotherapy every day this week and noticed slightly browner skin under my arm and a clear 'tan line' where the radiation stopped, but there was nothing on my breast and no soreness at all. The treatment became part of my morning routine. The receptionist got to know me and would sign me in and tell me which treatment machine I would be on without checking the paperwork.

I had a rest from running for a couple of days, but when I did go out, I felt a sharp pain in my left hip. It settled down as I walked, but after I'd been resting for a while, I would feel it as soon as I started moving again. I recognised the pain and concluded it was a hip bursa. I had overdone it at the weekend, and now I had an injury for my stubbornness. Fortunately, I had a massage booked for the following day, and if I took some Ibuprofen and rested it for a couple of days, I hoped it would quickly settle down. I had planned a 24-mile run along the Thames with Russ to celebrate our wedding anniversary, which I didn't want to miss.

Chapter 9 – Radiotherapy

I also had an appointment with Occupational Health to get some advice about returning to work. I saw a doctor I hadn't seen before, and he asked me to go through the whole period from my initial diagnosis through to the radiotherapy treatment. He took some notes and then asked, 'So, how are you emotionally?' I knew that question was likely to come. Being a logical person, I had dealt with my diagnosis and treatment by taking control of whatever I could and keeping up my exercise to prove that I was the one in charge. I wasn't about to break down and cry, but it did feel like the doctor was trying to get this from me. I just wanted to get back to work as normal, but with some leniency in case I experienced any extreme tiredness over the next month or so.

The doctor was aware that I had already returned to work with a flexible working pattern and didn't think he would be helping if he added a fixed structure to it. Instead, he suggested that my hours going forward should be discussed with my employer and we could look at reducing them. This wasn't what I wanted to do, but I did speak about it with my boss, who reminded me that I was entitled to request reduced hours at any time for 12 months without any impact on my future employment. I had forgotten about this and thought it would be helpful if in a few months' time I found I wasn't coping as well as I had hoped.

Sunday 5th August
We drove to Streatley, a village in Berkshire, where we had booked a hotel to celebrate our first wedding anniversary. This was where my Thames Ring 250 had started and where the Druid's Challenge, along the Ridgeway, passed through. It was also the starting point for the Autumn 100 in October. We had a hotel room with a patio that looked out towards the Thames, and the owners presented us with

a bottle of prosecco on ice to celebrate. We were still in the midst of a heatwave and the temperature was over 30 degrees, so we relished sitting outside in the late afternoon sunshine.

In the evening, we went out for a gorgeous dinner at a nearby restaurant. Our first 12 months as a married couple had been particularly challenging, but we were still celebrating a wonderful year together.

We got up late the next morning and sat by the river's edge having breakfast. It was idyllic and made me realise how little I had truly relaxed over the last few months, despite being off work since mid-March. Russ and I had not had the opportunity to have a break. It struck me then just how hard it had been, but at that moment, I felt sublime.

We set off on our 25-mile run with temperatures nearing 30 degrees. We ran from Goring to Day's Lock, heading towards Abingdon before turning back again. I was glad we were covering what would be the first leg of my Autumn 100-mile route, as it made me feel like I was really preparing for the event.

However, I was still worried about the pain in my hip. I felt nothing for the first 12.5 miles out to Day's Lock, but it started to twinge a little on the return. While it wasn't as bad as before, it didn't feel right.

Wednesday 8th August
My final radiotherapy session was followed by a review with a nurse. This was fairly routine. I didn't have much reddening of the skin, but I could still see the brown 'tan line' under my armpit where the radiation had been. The nurse warned me my skin was likely to get a little redder and advised me to continue using the E45 cream every day and to ring in if I had any issues.

I handed in the gown I had been given for the duration of my treatment and walked home. This time, I didn't feel any particular

Chapter 9 – Radiotherapy

sense of everything being over, I just got myself ready to return to the hospital for work that afternoon.

At work, we agreed to a phased return of no more than five hours a day for two weeks, with a review at the end of the month.

Despite my hip issues at the weekend, I decided to go for a run. I managed six miles, followed by five miles the following day with no issues. These were slow runs on a flat road to avoid causing any aggravation. I had a Parkrun planned for Saturday and a marathon on the Sunday. These would test both my hip and the rest of my body.

Chapter 10
Getting Back to Normal

Saturday 11th August
It was a beautiful morning as I drove to Southsea Seafront to take part in the Parkrun. Although aware that my body was finally getting back to its pre-cancer fitness, I started off at a comfortable pace. The last time I'd done this Parkrun was while recovering from my final chemotherapy treatment, when I'd found running at any sort of pace a challenge. This time, I ran strong to halfway and still felt strong. I decided to pick up the pace a bit. I felt invincible as I passed some other runners. It was so good to be back! I checked my time on my watch. It wasn't my fastest, but it was so much faster than I had done in a long while, and it was good to run in the knowledge I had no further treatment ahead. I chatted to a friend at the finishing line and broke down in tears of joy and relief.

The downside of this extra effort, however, was that I had aggravated my hip again, and by the end of the run it was hurting. As much as I was disappointed that I had a running injury to contend with, it did help me to reach the sensible decision not to run the marathon I had planned for the following day. It was a fairly hilly off-road one, which would make my hip worse. I hated the fact that my Autumn 100 training plan was going to be curtailed, and I worried whether I would be able to get enough training in, but I knew I had to give my hip the chance to heal.

Monday 13th August
It felt good to be back at work again. There had been times during chemotherapy when I couldn't imagine ever coming back because

Chapter 10 – Getting Back to Normal

I doubted how I would cope, but as time went on and my body recovered, I felt more confident and looked forward to my return. Doing fewer hours in the first instance made it harder in some ways, as I didn't have enough hours in which to finish everything. However, it was clear I did need the reduced hours, as when I got home and stopped for a while, I soon fell asleep from exhaustion. I also found that my tamoxifen medication brought on hot flushes, but so far these happened mostly at night. If this was the only side effect I was going to have to contend with then I could deal with it. I'd been told the side effects were at their worst in the first couple of months, as the body adjusted to the medication, so hopefully there would eventually be some improvement in their frequency and severeness.

I took up swimming to help maintain my fitness levels and went back to doing regular evening weight sessions. I could tell that I was getting my strength back. During the final cool down at one session, when I was crouched over on the floor in child's pose, a fierce wave of emotion came over me. Here I was doing what I had been doing in November 2017, before all this began, and I had made it through to the other side. It was all over. I was still alive, and everything was OK. I was back to doing exactly what I had been doing before. I lay there quietly sobbing to myself while the music played. I could at last get on with my life again, and everything would be back to how it should be. I composed myself when I stood up for the next set of cool down stretches, but when I went back into child's pose the same overwhelming emotions washed over me again, and I had to stifle a massive sob. I wasn't crying because I was sad. My sobs were from relief that it was finally over. I had made it. I may not be running now, but my life was so much more than running. I had used my sport of choice and the Autumn 100 as my focus to get me through chemotherapy, but now I didn't need that anymore. Hopefully, my injury would sort itself out and give me enough time to train sufficiently for the ultra race, but it wouldn't matter so much if it didn't, would it? There were plenty more runs I could do in the future.

Saturday 18th August
After resting my hip and not running during the week, I decided to try the Southsea Parkrun, but I was still uncomfortable. I knew my hip hadn't healed enough. If anything, it now felt worse. I was extremely disappointed and knew I would need an even longer break to give it a chance to improve.

The Autumn 100 had been the driving force to get me through my chemotherapy, but now this dream wasn't to become a reality. Russ advised me to see how I felt in a couple of weeks, but even though I agreed, deep down I knew I wouldn't have enough time to train sufficiently for such a demanding event. I knew I had trained well through my chemotherapy, but if I couldn't train now, it would be unwise to attempt 100 miles. My body was recovering from a severe battering, and although I had weathered the storm reasonably well, I had been told it would be months, possibly over a year, before I was fully back to my old self. Was this run important enough to risk my health at this time, when I could rest up and just pick another target?

During the Parkrun, my body ached all over. I had been pushing through the bad spells and fighting both mentally and physically for what seemed like ages. But I'd had enough of fighting. Perhaps now was the time to stop, recuperate and come back stronger.

Monday 20th August
I had my final appointment with my oncologist. She had looked at my blood results and determined I was postmenopausal. It may be that this was temporary and due to the chemotherapy, but as she wasn't certain she decided I should continue with the tamoxifen. I was to have no injections to supress my ovaries and no aromatase inhibitors

either. I didn't know much about these, but I was happy to do without based on my oncologist's advice if that meant less medication.

The poison that had passed through my body was dissipating and having far less of an effect on me. I could do some low intensity exercise on the rowing machine at the gym or go for a swim at my local pool. My hip was fine doing these forms of exercise.

Gradually, I went back to working my usual hours. My hair grew back to a level that looked relatively normal. The hip bursa did not seem to be healing and so I continued to swim. I finally went for some physio and ultrasound treatment. The recovery was achingly slow. I began to worry that perhaps there was something else going on, so I rang the breast cancer nurse, who tried to reassure me there really was nothing to worry about. My anxiety that the cancer would return was always lurking in the background.

I no longer had my running as therapy and began to struggle emotionally. After saying that I was back to normal, I really wasn't so sure. I felt more tired now compared to before all this happened, so the reduced exercise was probably helping with my recovery, but mentally I did not have the positive pick-me-up that an invigorating run would usually provide.

Monday 5th September
BBC journalist Rachael Bland, who presented on BBC Radio 5 Live, died today. She was diagnosed with breast cancer exactly one year to the day before me and set up the podcast, *You, Me and the Big C* with two other women who were also living with the disease. Rachael's death made me think about my own prognosis. What if the cancer came back with a vengeance? How long did I have left? Did I want to spend the rest of my time working towards a pension that I might not even get? What was the point? I discussed reducing my hours at work with Russ. He was happy for me to do whatever I felt was necessary.

I was worried that we wouldn't be able to afford it, but I spoke to my boss, who was happy for me to do fewer hours.

I spent some sleepless nights worrying about finances, but we agreed that I would start the reduced hours after we returned from our three-week holiday, which encompassed Russ doing Spartathlon, his dream race. The first week was probably going to be the most relaxed of the three. We were going to our friends' wedding in Rhodes, for which Russ was the best man. We had booked an apartment in Ancient Lindos, which was a short walk to St Paul's Bay, which I swam across for an hour each morning before breakfast. It helped me cope with the lack of running. Russ was doing very little training, as he was tapering for his big race. I was aware that even walking was a little uncomfortable for my hip, and I knew I had a long way to go until it healed sufficiently for me to go back to running. Not being able to do what I loved was frustrating, but swimming in the sea was a fantastic consolation.

The end of our trip to Rhodes meant a short flight to Athens, where Russ made his final preparations for Spartathlon. We stayed one night in Glyfada (where all the participants stay before the race) before picking up our crew from the airport the next day.

Friday 28th September

At 6am, Russ stood at the Acropolis of Athens waiting to start the historic Spartathlon race. We had attended the event several times to support others and now he was finally here to take part himself. He had earned his place by achieving the required time at a qualifying event and then being successful in the ballot. Russ's training had gone well, and he was familiar with the route and knew what to expect throughout the epic journey – or so he thought.

The weather is usually hot for the race, but this year it was going to be cool. It began to drizzle as he reached the marathon point, and

Chapter 10 – Getting Back to Normal

as the run progressed, this turned to wind and rain. Having come via a wedding in Rhodes, we weren't well enough prepared and hadn't packed enough dry clothes for him. Russ progressed up the mountain at 100 miles, but through the night he became colder and wetter and by morning he was chilled to the bone and really struggling to keep warm.

I saw messages on my phone from other crews who were further up the course to say that the weather was getting even worse. The entire region was being subjected to a Mediterranean hurricane known as a medicane. There was going to be no let up from the rain and increasing winds. Russ was now freezing, and his feet were covered in blisters. He was running slower and getting closer to the cut offs. Finally, at 117 miles, he was timed out and walked to the checkpoint, where we picked him up. He was shivering uncontrollably from the cold. Russ was devastated, and we were all gutted for him. We drove along the route towards the finish. The weather was atrocious. Anywhere else and the race would probably have been cancelled, but here in Greece it was still going on, and we passed other runners who were still battling through the storm. Seeing them only made matters worse for Russ. He had made it over the mountain at 100 miles, but we hadn't been sufficiently prepared for the extreme weather conditions. We'd learned lots of lessons, and Russ had an entry in for the following year, but we knew he was unlikely to get a place for a while, as the event is always oversubscribed.

After the race, we stayed in Sparta for a few days with the rest of our crew to recuperate. Timing out of the race was such a disappointment for Russ, but it was now time to fly to Cyprus so he could be best man yet again, this time at his son's wedding.

Whilst I was away, I took the momentous decision to enter the Canalslam for the following year. This involves running three long-distance events in relatively quick succession: the Grand Union Canal

Race in May, which Russ had run earlier in the year, the Kennet and Avon Canal Race at the end of July and the Liverpool to Leeds Canal Race on the late August Bank Holiday, which I had previously run in 2016. The mileage for each event is 145, 145 and 130 miles, respectively. I don't know what my initial impetus was, but I felt it was important to challenge myself, do things that scared me a little and push my boundaries. I was still injured, but there was plenty of time to heal. I was not going to be ready for the Autumn 100 this year, so the Canalslam would be my new goal.

Monday 15th October
After spending three weeks away, I went back to my physio treatment. There was some improvement, but I still wasn't ready to run, and it wasn't clear when this would be possible.

After having the pleasure of swimming in the sea whilst on holiday, it was difficult to get back to using the pool. I found it hard to get motivated. The Autumn 100 came and went. I had hoped I might be able to do at least 25 miles of the route, but I was still not ready to run any kind of distance. Perhaps the break would give my immune system the chance to recover properly. The running had served its purpose and got me through my chemotherapy treatment, but now my body needed time to recover fully, and I needed space to adjust to my usual hours at work. I was now at peace with the fact I couldn't run.

The hip bursar did gradually improve, and I was finally given the go ahead to spend some time at the gym on the cross trainer, where I could do some hip strengthening exercises. I was able to start running in November, initially just for 10 minutes on the treadmill. It was amazing to be able to run again and not feel the pain in my hip, but I knew I had to take it steady so as not to risk going back to square one.

I slowly increased my mileage, and by the end of December I was

Chapter 10 – Getting Back to Normal

able to run the last seven miles of the Portsmouth Coastal Marathon with Russ. He was struggling at this point, which was probably a good thing for me, as I doubt I would have been able to keep up otherwise. Seven miles was more than enough for me at that time.

In the new year, I began to get back to proper training. Russ was following a training plan for the Cyprus Marathon in March, so I decided to join him and do the same runs. I couldn't go at the same pace as him, but I could put in the same amount of effort.

I started my three-day working week at the beginning of December. We made a few changes and found that we were able to manage financially.

Wednesday March 2019

We flew to Cyprus for a holiday, and to run in the Paphos marathon. This was the third time I had run in this race, so I knew it well. The previous year, in between my surgery and starting the chemotherapy, we had come to Cyprus with our family, and I had run the 10k. This year, the weather was cool and dry but far windier than usual. I managed to finish in just over four hours, coming across the line barely able to stand and trying to control the increasingly painful cramps that had developed in my calves. My body clearly wasn't ready for running a marathon at pace. I had gone too hard in the first half, and the uncharacteristically strong winds hadn't helped either.

For the rest of the week, we settled down to relaxing and doing very little. The following weekend, we travelled along the coast to run the Limassol Marathon, which has a fast, flat course. Water stations had been set up every 2.5k, so I decided to walk for two minutes after arriving at each one and picking up a drink. I finished strong, in four hours 12 minutes, which really boosted my confidence. My training at this point, although not ready for running a hard marathon, was still good enough to provide a strong base for the next stage of my preparation for the Grand Union Canal Race when I got back to Portsmouth.

Saturday 25th May
I managed to stick to the training plan I wrote for the Grand Union Canal Race. After gradually increasing my mileage, three weeks before the event I reached a peak of 70 miles. I also practised my run/walk strategy and my race nutrition.

The race started at 6am, and I quickly got myself into a comfortable pace to while away the miles. From 65 miles onwards, I was allowed to have buddy runners for moral support, and I was fortunate to have several volunteers. Although there were many times when I was not in the mood for conversation, it was good to share the experience with close friends and to chat when I felt up to it.

By the following morning, an all-consuming tiredness had come over me, and it was hard to keep myself going (not surprising since I had been up and moving constantly for over 24 hours), but my buddies kept spurring me along. At this point, I was walking briskly and not really running at all. I had my phone with me and rang a few other friends along the way. They gave me so much encouragement, and I could feel myself welling up with emotion as I realised I was actually going to finish the race. The cut off was 45 hours, and I was hoping to finish in under 35. But as I got closer to the finish, achieving my goal seemed unlikely, as my legs hurt all over. However, in the last few miles, I managed to find the strength to run a little, and I finished the race in 34 hours and 47 minutes, finishing in 13th place overall and second female. Russ had my chocolate 'Screw Cancer' trophy from Ellen ready and waiting, and we smashed it open and began eating it to celebrate. I had been saving it for over 16 months for this special day... the day when I could finally say that I had come out the other side of a breast cancer diagnosis and treatment. I was back to running as strong as ever – perhaps even stronger than I had ever been.

Chapter 10 – Getting Back to Normal

My experience with breast cancer has changed my perspective on life in many ways. If I hadn't had cancer, I probably wouldn't have entered the Canalslam. In the end, I missed out on the slam as I pulled out of the Kennet and Avon Canal Race at 122 miles after passing out on the course due to becoming dehydrated and disorientated. However, only four weeks later, I still managed to complete the Liverpool to Leeds 130-mile race. Before cancer, perhaps I would have given up after realising I wasn't going to finish the Canalslam, but my new approach was not to wallow in self-pity but to get straight back up and battle through to the next race.

Monday 10th February 2020
Unfortunately, Russ didn't manage to secure a place in Spartathlon 2019, but we still went and followed the event, which was my seventh year there. Although I loved watching the race as a spectator, I never imagined I would be good enough to compete in it. I would watch the changing emotions of the runners as they battled with the heat (and occasionally the rain!) and the harsh cut offs. Even the elite athletes still struggled to finish, and I didn't like running in the heat at the best of times. I used to love seeing the runners coming towards the finishing line with all the local schoolchildren riding their bikes alongside them. They would be holding up their national flag with pride as they made their way along the final main street with everybody cheering them on. The finishing custom was for the runners to kiss the left foot of the statue of the Spartan king Leonidas. Despite their exhaustion, I would always notice the overwhelming joy on their faces.

Having proclaimed I would never do the race, I now questioned my motive for doing so. I recalled how I'd felt after finishing the Thames Ring 250, and I recognised the emotions the runners were feeling as they made their life-changing memories. This is what life should be about. I had assumed I would never get a qualifier, but I had just managed to get one at GUCR. I finally realised and acknowledged that my reasons for not wanting to do Spartathlon were because I feared the race and didn't want to enter if I wasn't good enough to finish. I questioned what I was so scared about. I had a qualifier now, so why not put my name in the hat and see if I got in? The worst that could happen was being timed out, but I was still alive after going through cancer treatment, so why not get on and live life to the fullest by doing the things that scared me? I could experience Spartathlon for myself rather than watching it from the sidelines. Before I could change my mind, I put my name down for Spartathlon 2020.

Neither Russ nor I were successful in the ballot in 2020, so we applied again for the following year. Then Spartathlon 2020 was cancelled due to the pandemic and all accepted entrants that year were rolled over to 2021, so the next time we could apply was in February 2022, which we duly did.

In March 2022, the unthinkable happened and Russ and I were both selected in the Spartathlon ballot. It was time to start training!

Chapter 11
THIS IS SPARTA!

Friday September 30th 2022

I stepped off the coach into the dark and followed Russ through the car park and up the stairs to join the rapidly increasing throng of people at the Acropolis. We found a spot amongst the crowds and chatted nervously with our UK teammates. I looked up at the Parthenon, in all its splendour, lit up by the many lights strategically positioned around its base. My emotions were mixed. I had been coming here every year since 2013. I had watched many friends begin their 154-mile Spartathlon journey from this point. I had cheered them along from beginning to end, congratulated those who had finished and commiserated with those who had been timed out by the tight cut offs. Now it was my turn. This had been a long time coming.

I felt calmer than I had expected to be. I had trained as well as I could and stuck to my plan. My father's health had been deteriorating, but I still managed to find the time to visit him and ensure he had everything he needed. In March, he had become bedbound and was visited four times a day by carers. On the morning of 12th July 2022, he caught an infection that finally got the better of him. He was taken into hospital, where I watched him take his final breath. Although I had to spend time clearing his flat and preparing for his funeral, it released me from the worry of leaving him behind when I travelled to Greece. While going through his things, I found a sunhat, which I decided I would wear for the race if it was sunny. I also chose to wear the watch he'd been wearing when he died. Now I felt my dad would be able to join me on my journey in spirit.

I stood at the beginning of the route with the other runners as we had our pictures taken. As the start time loomed ever closer, I was aware of the increasing congestion as we all shuffled forward to get closer to the starting banner. From where I was standing, I couldn't even see the start, as there were too many people blocking my view, but I knew where it was. Previously I had been standing on the opposite side of the banner down the hill a little, ready with my camera to take pictures of everyone as they rushed past. This time I was taking on this momentous journey myself, and this time I would be waving at those cheering and taking pictures of me along the route. I had already lost sight of Russ. We had agreed to run our own races and not stay together.

I heard the starting horn distinctly above the murmur of the nervous participants. Nothing happened for a moment, and then gradually I could see the slow shuffle of feet moving forwards as the runners in front of me set off. Very soon there was enough space to run normally, and I found myself running down the hill from the Acropolis towards the busy roads of Athens City Centre. The police had temporarily stopped the traffic so that we could run freely, and on busier roads that were still open, there were coned-off sections to the side to keep us relatively safe. The pace was comfortable. It was important to keep a pace that was fast enough to stay ahead of the cut offs while slow enough not to overdo it and burn out. Very quickly the darkness made way for dawn as the sun began to rise. Today and tomorrow this region of Greece was going to be experiencing a heatwave. My dad's hat was in my hand for now, but I would be needing it soon enough, and I smiled at my fated find.

The first place I was looking forward to reaching was the half marathon point at Elefsina. I ran through the town, dodging the busy Friday morning traffic and passing the coffee shop on my right, where every year previously I had stood with a drink cheering

Chapter 11 – This is Sparta!

everyone on. Today I could see two people standing on the corner wearing the easily distinguishable bright red UK crew shirts. It was my crew cheering and taking photographs of everyone in the team as they passed. After focusing on my initial pacing, I now relaxed a little. I smiled and waved back. I was finally here, after all these years, running the race that previously I had never felt good enough to enter. Having breast cancer had changed all that. I was doing the race I was never going to do, and I was loving it. I would next see my crew again at the marathon point at Megara, where they were allowed to provide assistance. They had my plan, which included details of what I wanted to eat and drink.

I passed an oil refinery. I had never smelt the fumes before when driving past in a crew car, but now I embraced the aroma, thankful that I was finally here to inhale the noxious fumes for myself.

As the morning progressed, the temperature rose to the mid-thirties and my dad's hat became my saviour. Every time I reached a checkpoint, I would soak it in a bucket of water to help keep me cool. At Megara, my crew filled my neck buff with ice and provided me with fuel and encouragement. I was ahead of the cut offs, and everything was going according to plan. The next time I would see my crew again was just after the Corinth Canal at 50 miles. Once I got there, the cut offs eased a little and I could run a little slower. I continued to run along the coastal road, with the inviting sparkling waters of the Megara Gulf on my left. Fortuitously, Russ and I found each other along the route, and I was grateful to be able to run with him for a short while. We were near the back of the race, and we found that some of the checkpoints had already run out of water. Combined with the steadily climbing temperatures there was evidence of some runners already struggling with cramp. I too began to struggle with cramping and had to keep stopping to stretch out my tight calf. I continued with my stop/start running until I found myself approaching the Corinth Canal. There was a long climb on the road that led up to it, and I was distracted by trying to catch my first sight of the huge chasm that had been cut through the land, initially to provide a shortcut for cargo ships but now no longer of any significant economic importance. I reached the narrow pedestrian footpath over the canal and could see the sheer cliffs down to the water on my left. A huge wave of emotion engulfed me. I had been over this footpath so many times but never as a competitor. My eyes welled up with tears. I wiped them away and continued with a massive grin on my face. It was another mile until I reached the checkpoint. Here there was a coach filled with runners who had already pulled out or missed the cut off because of the heat or injuries. I crossed the timing mat and hugged the checkpoint signpost, which showed how far we had come and the cut off time. I had made it here inside the required nine and a half hours. I had enough time to go to the toilet and eat and drink with my crew before continuing. From now on, the checkpoints would be closer together. I had eight miles until I reached Ancient Corinth and saw my crew again.

Everything seemed quieter now, and the busy streets and roads had been replaced by narrower paths straddled by dusty crop fields. I was relieved that I could now run at a slower pace. I knew the cramps had affected me. My legs ached far more than they should at this stage, and I doubted I could run any faster than I was currently going. The miles slowly ticked by, and as I got closer to Ancient Corinth, I began to recognise the streets around me. I had been here so many times before. For a short while, I forgot how tired I was, and my pace picked up as I turned the final corner down the slope with the striking ancient ruins ahead of me and the bustling high street full of restaurants and tourist shops to my right. Despite my weary legs, I continued to grin from ear to ear. To reach this point in the race was a massive achievement.

Chapter 11 – This is Sparta!

It was now late afternoon and still extremely warm, but it would be cooling down a little as darkness descended. I set off again, eating the ice cream that my crew had bought me. I would see them next at approximately 100k. As I left, Russ arrived at the checkpoint behind me. The ice cream followed by an orange juice did not sit well in my stomach, and I struggled for a while to get back into my stride. By the time I reached my crew again, I knew I was closer to the cut offs, but they were still encouraging and positive about how I was getting on. I put on my reflective gear and lights, as I knew it would be dark soon, and quickly set off, conscious of not taking any more time than I needed to.

I continued running but soon found that I needed to be sick, and I retched a few times on the roadside. This made me feel a little better, but I knew that I was now moving too slowly, and I was losing the small time buffer that I had left. Abruptly it was dark, and I could see very little around me. Just the occasional runner as they passed me with their headlights on. From behind me I heard the words, 'Is that my gorgeous wife I see?'

Russ had caught me up, and he sounded cheerful. I told him I was struggling to run, and that I expected to be timed out at the next crew checkpoint at Halkion. He said his quads were wrecked, just like mine, and his progress was also slow, but he was still running. I told him to keep going so as not to miss the cut off too. My torch shone on his reflective gear, and I watched as he disappeared around a bend in the road ahead, figuring that it would be the last time I saw him until the end of the race. I expected to be timed out soon, but Russ looked strong to me. My mind began to wander, and I started to think about my dad. My sports watch had nearly run out of battery but my dad's faithful analogue watch on my other wrist was still going strong. It was just after 9pm. I looked up at the myriad stars visible in the clear night sky. They took my breath away. I marvelled at the vastness of the space above me and its natural beauty. This felt like it was the perfect time and place to talk to my dad. I said to him, 'I hope I make you proud' and I told him that I had done my best and that we had shared an amazing journey together, but now it was time to say goodbye as my journey was about to come to an end. I was convinced that I would not reach Halkion before the cut off. In my own small world, I wandered aimlessly up the hill in the dark. I had not eaten or drunk enough recently, and my energy levels were at rock bottom. I knew there were no more runners behind me, and I was all ready to hand in my number when I reached the checkpoint.

I walked silently on in solitary reflection ready to accept my fate and the end of my adventure, but it was not meant to be. From the darkness ahead of me, I heard shouting.

'Come on, come on. You've got two minutes to get to the checkpoint. You can do it!'

I looked up and saw the indistinct shapes of people coming towards me. There was a timing mat that I needed to cross before the cut off. The shouts of encouragement were deafening, and they disturbed my solitary thoughts. I had been walking uphill for quite some time, but I knew I'd have to run to get to the checkpoint in time. I shuffled forwards as fast as my tired, exhausted, aching body would let me, whilst focusing on the excited shouts of encouragement alongside me. There was a tremendous cheer when I finally crossed the timing mat with barely a minute to spare. I was too tired to think, and I was slurring my words. My crew gave me some milk to drink and pushed me quickly out of the checkpoint, telling me it was all downhill towards the next one. I was now more alert and ready to continue, and I found myself shuffling slowly down the hill. Thoughts of my dad were gone for now; I had a job to do. I had about half an hour to get to the next checkpoint, but I'd lost all concept of time. I couldn't afford to stop to eat or drink – I just had to keep moving forward. I

Chapter 11 – This is Sparta!

knew there were only two more checkpoints until I got to Ancient Nemea, the halfway point, and this gave me renewed focus. I was determined to reach it. I ran when I could, and although it was not particularly fast, it was quicker than my walking pace. I reached the next checkpoint and ran straight past it, fearful that if I stopped, I would be pulled from the race. I thought I might be behind the cut off, but they let me through, which meant I would be allowed to continue the race. I kept moving forwards. It seemed to be mostly uphill, and I found that I was struggling to run. I knew what time the cut off was at Ancient Nemea, and I looked at my dad's watch and realised I wasn't going to make it. I heard a cheer in the distance. I expected this was for another runner who had just managed to squeeze inside the cut off. I was certain that my race would be over at the next checkpoint and decided to simply enjoy these last few solitary minutes out on the course and relish my final moments as part of one of the most gruelling and historic races in the world.

I reached the checkpoint and saw that the timing mat had already been removed. Everything was being cleared up save for a few chairs where a single runner was being tended to. It took me a few moments to realise it was Russ in the chair. Despite my tiredness, I gave him a big smile. I was really pleased to see him, although it meant that he too had been timed out. We had run our separate races, but they had both ended at the same point. I had managed to reach halfway and was grateful for having had the opportunity to run in this most iconic race. I had not been good enough to finish but I had tried my best, and the memories made would stay with me always.

We were driven to our team hotel for the night and relaxed while other members of the UK team continued their journey to the finish, where they would finally kiss the foot of the statue of Leonidas in Sparta. I did not see anyone finish this year, but I still had my memories from previous visits and of watching the faces of runners coming down the last stretch towards the statue. The significance of the finish was always clear in their faces, but this year, the finish was not to be for me or Russ.

I had no regrets about taking part in the race. I felt that I had done my best and I was proud of what I had achieved. However, after Spartathlon, I found that I lost my enthusiasm for running for a while. I probably just needed a rest. I would find another event soon enough that would rekindle my love for all things running.

So now I choose to do the things that scare me and the things I think I cannot do. Without knowing what is around the corner, I don't want to look back at my life and think, *I wish I'd done that* or, *What if?* Life is for living, so I'm going to make sure that I go out and live it.

Epilogue

January 2023

'Only those who will risk going too far can possibly find out how far one can go.' – T.S. Eliot

It's over five years since my original diagnosis of breast cancer. I have had five years of mammograms, MRI scans and tamoxifen medication. After this time, the breast cancer nurse rang to let me know I would have no more appointments with the hospital, and I was being discharged to my GP. I was disappointed to find out that I would need to continue taking the tamoxifen for yet another five years. I would now have a routine mammogram every three years as part of the UK breast screening programme, just like every other woman over 50. Perhaps now should have been a time for celebration, however, I felt uncomfortable at the prospect of having lost my security blanket of routine annual checkups. It had been good to get some reassurance each year that everything was still OK, and that the cancer had not returned.

Somehow, the worry that the cancer might come back never fully leaves you, but you learn how to live with it. You return to work as before and life goes on, but your cancer journey is never really over. When I look at my right arm, I can see the evidence of my damaged veins from the chemotherapy drugs. My left breast is more uplifted than my right as a result of the surgery to remove my tumour. I can still see the scar under my left armpit, and I must remember to spray deodorant under my right arm first or else I will put too much on because I no longer have any feeling there. There are still three small tattoos on my upper body from the radiotherapy treatment I underwent. These are the constant reminders of my cancer journey.

My body and mind may have changed, but I will continue to strive to look for the positives. After all, I am still here. I am grateful for the life I still have, complete with its highs and lows, and for the friends and family around me. I have discovered that perhaps I am stronger than I thought I was, something that Russ has often said. Perhaps we all have this strength inside us when we can focus enough to reach our goals. You cannot control how cancer will affect you personally. The cancer may still return over the course of the next few years, but I don't have to sit around moping about it or let it take control of my life. I have a strong, healthy, active body, and I will continue to take each wonderful day as it comes. Yes, I will keep on stressing about insignificant things that I really shouldn't stress about, but this is who I am. The one constant that kept me focused and helped me to get through the treatment and out the other side was my regular exercise, even if it was just going out for a walk. Exercise was my therapy and my meditation throughout my journey, and I expect it will continue to be this way for many years to come.

In fact, my love of long distance running led me to enter the 'Centurion Running' Autumn 100 mile race in October 2023. This was the race I had planned to run in 2018 and was my goal that had kept me focused throughout my treatment. However, injury had prevented me from reaching the start line. Exactly five years on, I finally ran and completed the Autumn 100. It was touch and go as to whether I would finish as I was still recovering from an illness, and when I finally reached the finish line I cried with relief. Not just for finishing but also for completing the race I had originally planned to do over five years ago.

Epilogue

As time continues to pass, I am aware that I am getting older and slower, and perhaps I should be taking it a bit easier, but I'm not quite ready for that yet. After saying 'Never again!' I have decided to enter the Thames Ring 250-mile race. I am back out running along the Thames Path, the Grand Union Canal and the Oxford Canal, revisiting the more difficult parts with good friends, stopping for coffee and cake and having a good laugh while trying to ensure that we know the route well enough so we don't get lost during the actual event. For me, running is not just about the destination, although it is great to get to the end. It is also about the journey to reach that goal and the memories made along the way, and I'm lucky enough to still have time to make a few more special memories before I hang up my ultra running shoes for good.

Acknowledgements

As I write this, I realise how lucky I am to have so many friends around me that have supported me through my cancer treatment. Some ran or walked with me, some came along and sat with me through my chemotherapy. Others gave me homemade dinners to put in my freezer or a box of goodies to help me through my treatment. Although the number of well-wishers was overwhelming at times, I'm fortunate to have been blessed with so many good friends. A special mention goes out to Angie Agate, Sarah Dryden, Russ Bestley, Mich and Amy Hardie, Emma Bird, Alex Meek, Claire Flemming, Katie Carew-Robinson, Tony Hewitt, Ellen Cottom, Len Turrell, Beth Pirie, Lisa Hewitt, Emma Baker, Sarah Kell and Iaan Davies. You all made a difficult period in my life far easier to deal with. Thank you from the bottom of my heart for all your support.

A big thank you to my husband, Russ, for always being there for me. For encouraging me to get my story published, for his positivity throughout, and for believing in me when I often doubted myself.

To James Elson, founder of Centurion Running and a good friend. Your support as Russ's coach over the years has meant so much; more than you could ever know. Thank you for your thoughtful and insightful words in the foreword to this book. I'm truly grateful.

To Alexa Whitten from The Book Refinery Ltd, who, over the last five years, has kept in touch and helped me to move forward towards a finished product, and to Danielle, my editor, who has helped turn my musings into something that is more structured and coherent.

Acknowledgements

Finally, and most significantly, a massive thank you to our wonderful NHS and the staff at the Queen Alexandra Hospital in Portsmouth. Special thanks in particular to those in the Breast Screening, Radiology, Surgery, Chemotherapy and Radiotherapy departments. You are angels in disguise. Without the NHS and its hardworking, caring and compassionate staff, I would not be here today.

My hope is that this book might help others who are going through something similar, to find their path through, what can be, one of the most traumatic and difficult periods in life. To keep moving forward each day, every day, one day at a time.